Science made easy

Key Stage 2
Ages 7–8

Authors David Evans, Mike Evans,
Linda Ellis and Hugh Westrup
Consultants Sean McArdle and Kara Pranikoff

Certificate ☆ ☆ ☆ ☆

Congratulations to ....
(write your name here)
for successfully finishing this book.

☆ *You're a star!* ☆

DK

Is it alive?

Science facts

All living things have seven processes in common. Every living thing can **M**ove, **R**eproduce, and is **S**ensitive to the world around it. Each one can also **G**row, **R**espire (use the gases in air), **E**xcrete (get rid of waste from its body) and use food by a process called **N**utrition. To help you remember the processes, put the first letter of each one together to spell **MRS GREN**.

Science quiz

The words below describe the seven life processes of living things. Draw a line from each word to the picture that shows it happening.

Reproduces
Excretes
Respires
Grows
Nutrition
Sensitive
Moves

Science activity

Which is the most sensitive part of your body? Collect some objects, such as coins, toys or vegetables. With your eyes shut, can you tell which object is which using your toes? How well can you feel the objects with your elbows?

Are plants alive?

Science facts

Plants are living things, but they are different from animals. Plants make their own food inside their leaves. They make the food using sunlight, gas from the air, and water from the soil. They use this food to grow. Plants can reproduce to make new plants. Unlike animals, plants do not move from place to place, but they are sensitive to light and always grow towards it.

Science quiz

Here are some facts about an oak tree. Put a tick (✔) beside any fact that tells you the oak tree is alive.

- ☐ The leaves of the tree make food.
- ☐ Birds nest in the branches.
- ☐ It takes in water through its roots.
- ☐ The branches move in the wind.
- ☐ It produces acorns in autumn.
- ☐ Squirrels eat the acorns.
- ☐ It grows 300 mm each year.

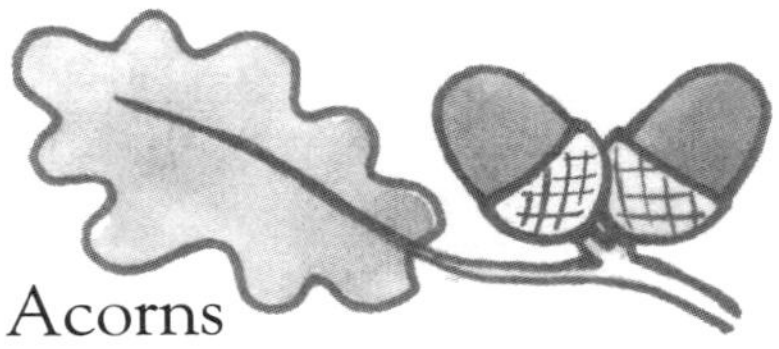

Science activity

(!) Put a few acorns or seeds in a flowerpot with some soil or compost. Water them regularly. Make sure they get plenty of light. Eventually, each one may sprout a shoot. What happens if you keep on watering the shoots? How can you tell if they are alive?

How do plants stay healthy?

Science facts

Plants make their own food. They take gas from the air and water from the soil to make sugar and starch. Chlorophyll allows plants to absorb sunlight, gives plants their green colour, and helps them make their food. A plant's roots take water from the soil. There are special minerals in the water that help the plant grow and stay healthy.

Science quiz

Andrew wanted to find out the best way to grow cress. He took three dishes, put cotton wool in each one and sprinkled cress seeds over the cotton wool. He put dishes **A** and **B** on a window ledge and dish **C** in a dark cupboard. He watered dishes **A** and **C** every day, but not dish **B**. This is how the dishes looked after two weeks. Label each dish **A**, **B** or **C** to show which is which.

Dish ....
The seeds have not grown.

Dish ....
The seedlings have long, weak stems and small, pale-yellow leaves.

Dish ....
The seedlings have strong stems and large, dark-green leaves.

Science activity

Place some cress seeds on cotton wool in two dishes. Put one dish in the refrigerator and the other on a window ledge. Water them regularly. What do you think will happen to the seeds in each dish, and why?

Are all roots the same?

Science facts

Plants use their roots to hold themselves in the soil. The other main job of a root is to take in water from the soil. The plant uses the water to make its food. Some roots go down a long way into the soil to find water. Other roots spread out widely to use water all around them. The roots of some plants become very fat because the plant stores food in them.

Science quiz

Mina likes helping her mother in the garden. One of her favourite jobs is pulling up weeds. Here are some weeds that she found.

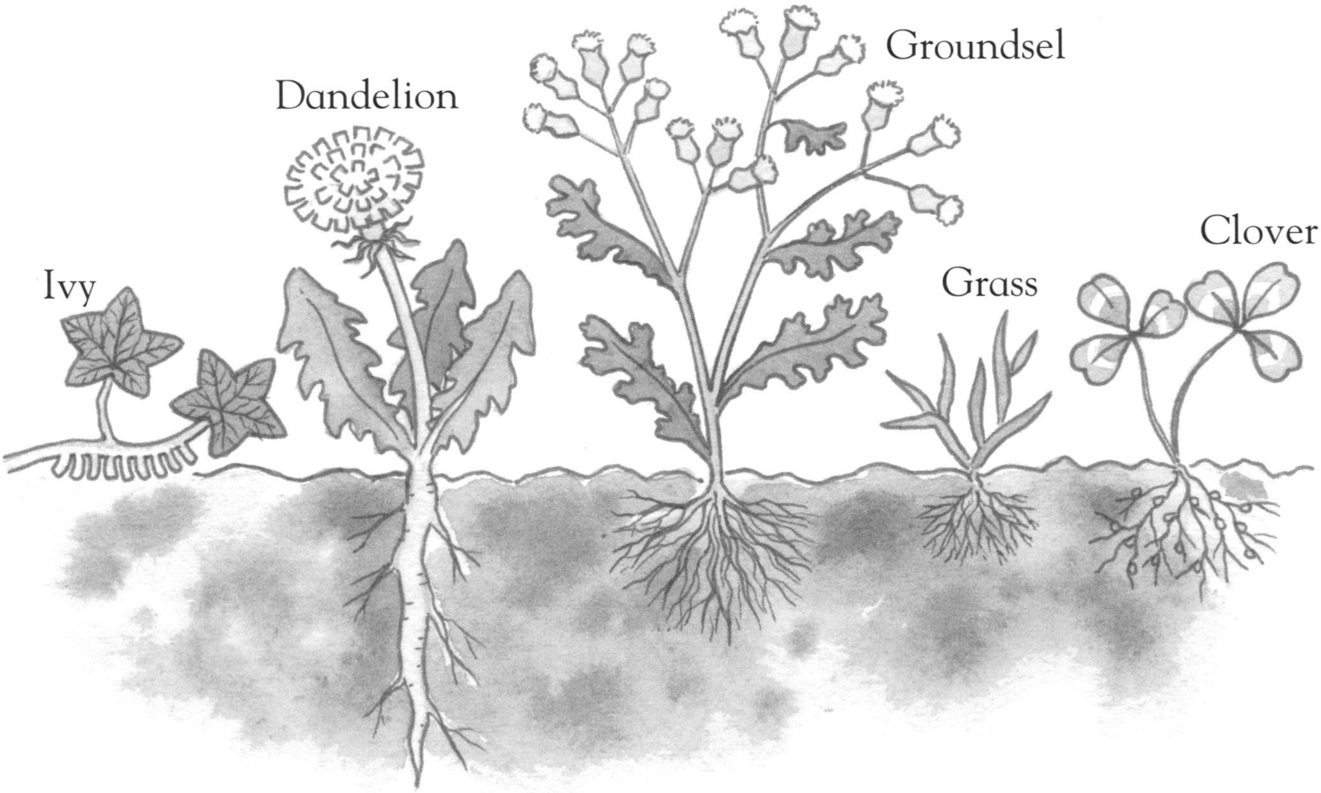

Why is dandelion the hardest to pull up?..

Why is ivy the easiest to pull up? ....

Science activity

Some of the vegetables that we eat are swollen plant roots. How many different root vegetables can you find in your local greengrocer's or supermarket?

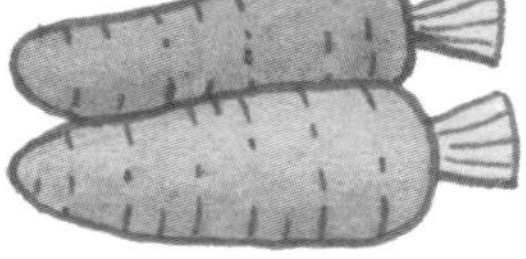

Are all leaves the same?

Science facts

Leaves are usually green because they have a green chemical inside them called chlorophyll, which catches sunlight. They also have tiny holes on their surface to let air and water in and out. Leaves use sunlight, air and water to make food.

Science quiz

Use this branching Yes/No key to find out what tree each leaf comes from.

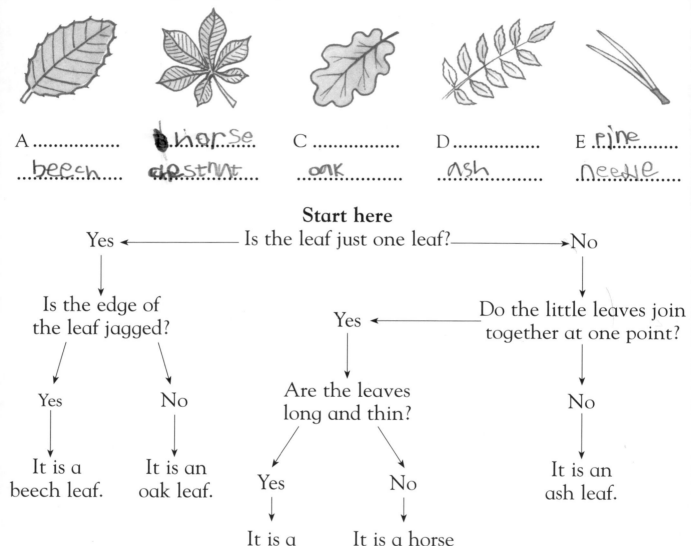

A .... beech

B horse chestnut

C .... oak

D .... ash

E pine needle

Start here

Is the leaf just one leaf?
- Yes → Is the edge of the leaf jagged?
  - Yes → It is a beech leaf.
  - No → It is an oak leaf.
- No → Do the little leaves join together at one point?
  - Yes → Are the leaves long and thin?
    - Yes → It is a pine needle.
    - No → It is a horse chestnut leaf.
  - No → It is an ash leaf.

Science activity

(!) Make a collection of leaves from your garden or local park. Can you sort the leaves into different groups? What features do the leaves in each group have in common?

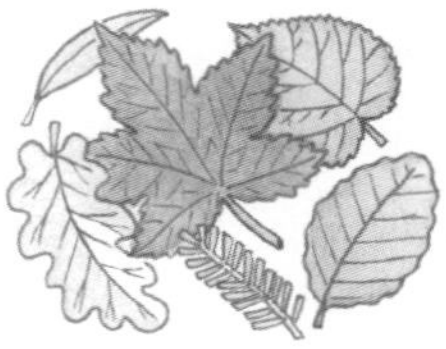

What do plants do with water?

Science facts

All plants have roots that perform two functions. Firstly, they anchor the plant to the ground. Secondly, they absorb water from the soil. Dissolved chemicals in the water, called nutrients, are needed for healthy plant growth. Plants also need water to make their food. Water is carried from the roots, through thin tubes in the stems, to every part of the plant. When the water reaches the surface of the leaves, it evaporates, causing more water to travel up the stem.

A small plastic bag tied around the leaf of a plant shows how water evaporates from the leaves. After a few hours in a sunny place, tiny water droplets form on the inside of the bag.

Science quiz

Gordon cut all the roots off a broad-bean plant and planted it in a flowerpot. He continued to water the plant, but after two days it started to wilt and after four days it was dead. Explain why this happened.

....

....

....

Science activity

(!) Take two stalks of celery with a small amount of root. Remove the leaves from one stalk. Put the stalks in coloured water (use food colouring) and leave them for two days. Ask an adult to help you slice through one of the stalks about 3 cm from the bottom. Draw a picture of the pattern that you see. How far has the coloured water travelled up each stalk? Is there a difference? Why?

Do all plants have flowers?

Science facts

Most plants produce seeds that grow into new plants. The seeds of conifer trees grow inside woody cones. The seeds of other plants grow inside flowers. Ferns and mosses have neither cones nor flowers. Instead, they have special parts that produce tiny specks called spores, which grow into new plants.

Science quiz

Some of the plants in the pictures below are flowering plants. Circle the flowers.

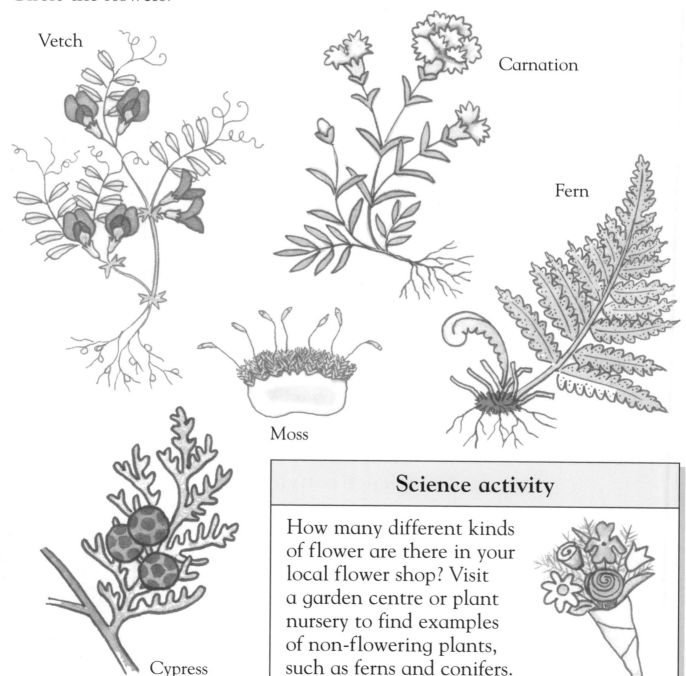

Vetch

Carnation

Fern

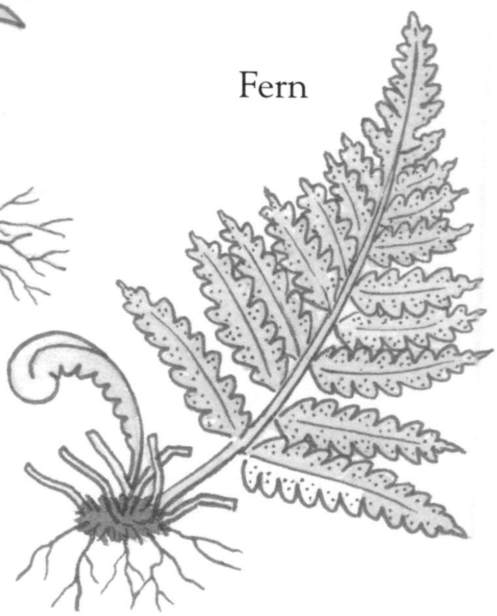

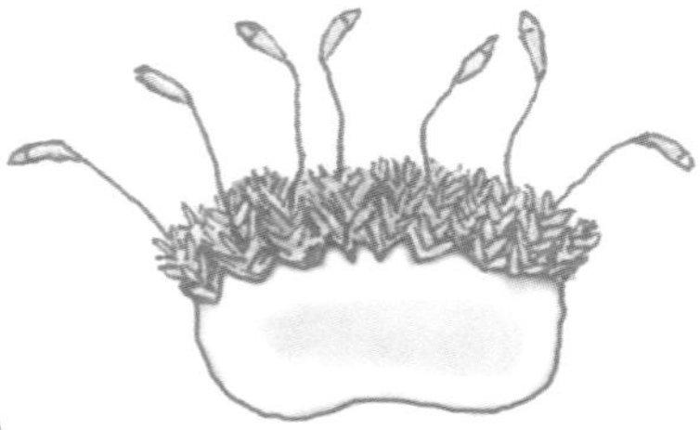

Moss

Cypress

Science activity

How many different kinds of flower are there in your local flower shop? Visit a garden centre or plant nursery to find examples of non-flowering plants, such as ferns and conifers.

What kind of seed is it?

Science facts

Seeds germinate (sprout) to grow into new plants. Many seeds grow inside flowers. Fruits then form around some seeds to protect them. There are many different kinds of fruit, some of which we eat. We eat nuts as well, which are seeds with a hard, woody shell. Some children are allergic to nuts. If they eat nuts they get very sick. Always ask an adult before you eat nuts.

Science quiz

Which seed comes from which fruit? Draw a line from each fruit to its seed.

A 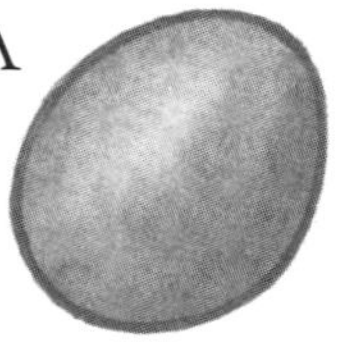

B 

C 

D 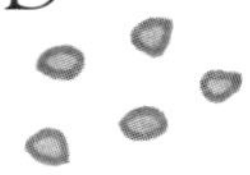

E 

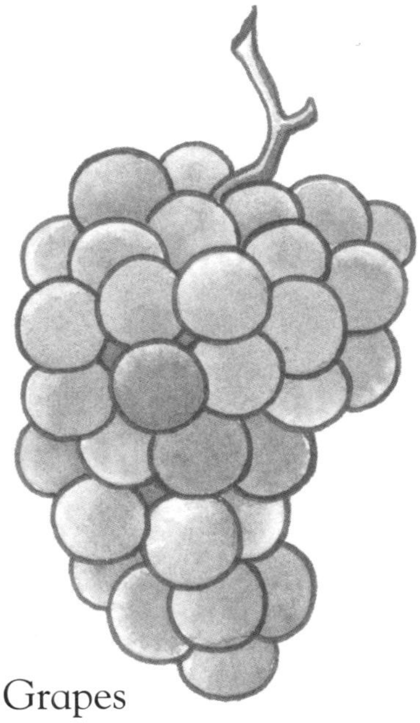

Grapes

Apple

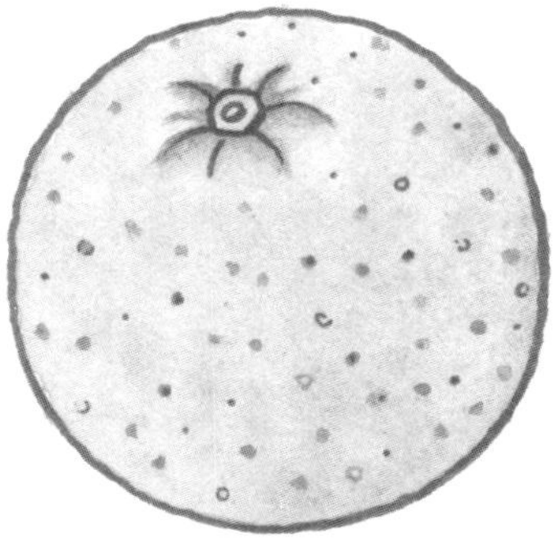

Orange

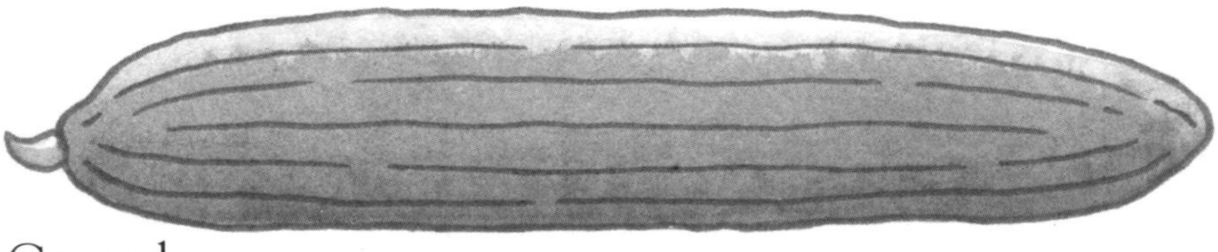

Cucumber

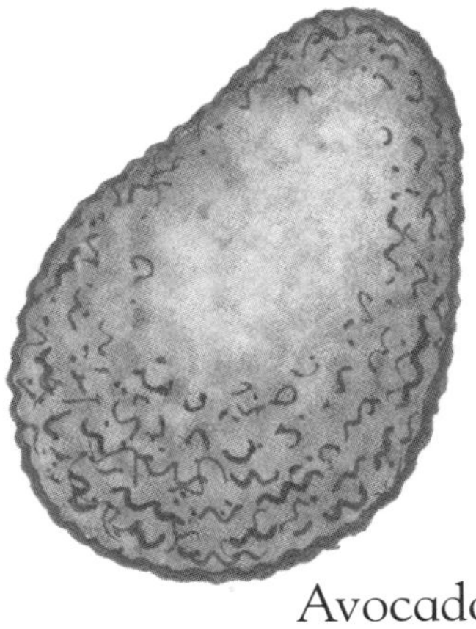

Avocado

Science activity

(!) How many different kinds of seed are there in a packet of birdseed? Sort them into groups. What is different about each group? Which seeds do birds prefer?

How do seeds grow in new places?

Science facts

A plant produces many seeds. If all the seeds fell to the ground around a parent plant, they would choke each other when they started to grow. Seeds are adapted so that they can be dispersed as widely as possible. Some are suited to being dispersed by the wind and others by water. Seeds inside juicy fruits are dispersed after being eaten by birds and other animals.

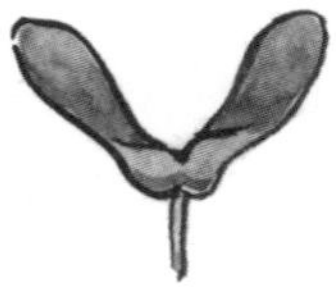

Sycamore seeds are dispersed by wind.

Apple seeds are usually dispersed by animals.

Coconut seeds are dispersed by water.

Science quiz

Look at the seeds below. In the boxes, write **W** for those that are dispersed by wind and **A** for those dispersed by animals.

Blackberry ☐

Cherry ☐

Dandelion ☐

Pine cone ☐

Explain how an apple seed might be dispersed by water.

....

....

Science activity

Collect some sycamore seeds or ash keys. These seeds are particularly well suited to wind dispersal. Compare how long each takes to fall to the ground. Does the length of the wings on the seeds make a difference?

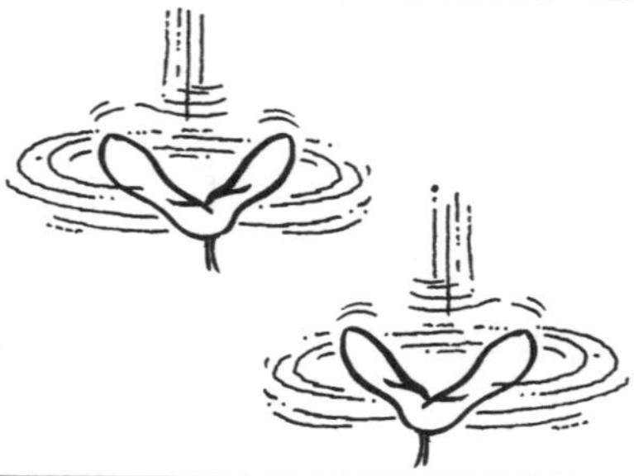

What do seeds need to grow?

Science facts

Seeds need water to germinate and grow into new plants. Some seeds need to be kept in a warm place before they will start to grow, while others germinate best if they are kept cool.

Science quiz

Here are a number of beans that have been planted in different ways.

Bean A is planted in sand but not watered.

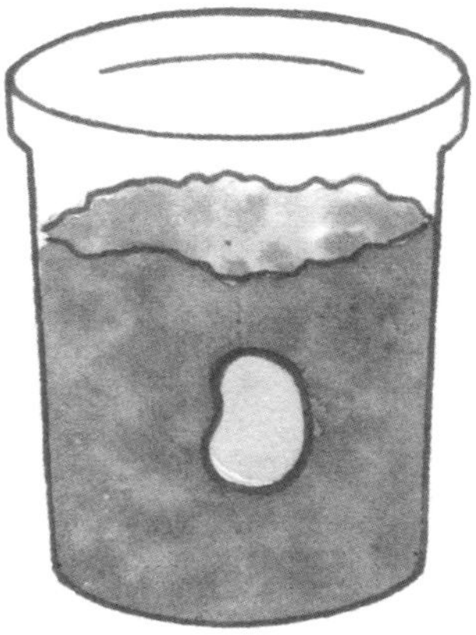

Bean B is planted in soil and watered every day.

Bean C is planted in soil but not watered.

Bean D is planted on cotton wool and watered every day.

Bean E has no soil or water.

Which beans do you think will grow?

....

Why did you make this choice?

....

....

Science activity

(!) A packet of birdseed contains many different types of seed. Plant each type in a different flowerpot. Put the same amount of soil in each pot and add a little water each day. Which type of seed germinates best?

Can food keep you healthy?

Science facts

Living things need food and water to stay alive. Foods such as milk, meat, fish, eggs and nuts contain proteins that help you grow. Other foods, such as fruit, bread and pasta, contain carbohydrates that give you energy to move and play. Fats, such as butter and margarine, also give you energy. Fruits and vegetables contain vitamins and minerals that keep you healthy.

Science quiz

Here are some of the foods that Jason found in his kitchen. He read the labels to find out which foods contain fats and which contain proteins.

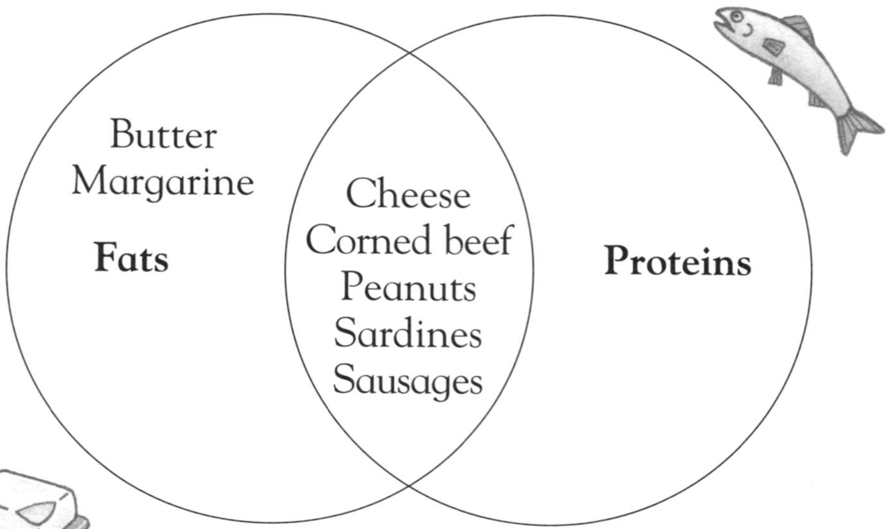

Do any of the foods contain mainly fats?
If so, which ones?

....

....

Do any of the foods contain mainly proteins?
If so, which ones?

....

....

Which foods will help Jason to grow?

....

....

Science activity

Each can or packet of food has a label that tells you how much protein, carbohydrate, fat and vitamins there are in 100 grams of the food. Which food in your kitchen contains the most carbohydrate?

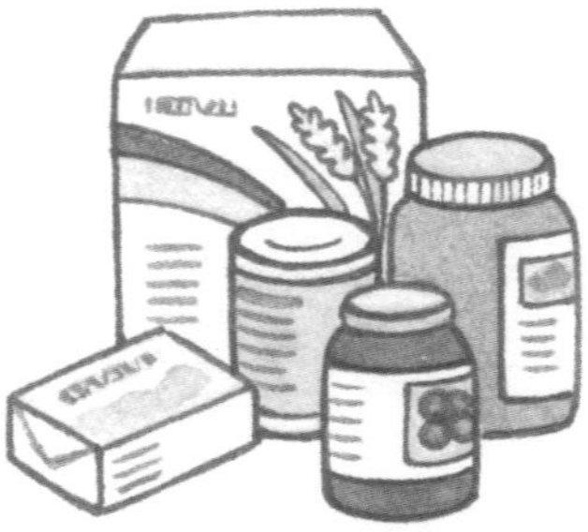

What do animals eat?

Science facts

Many animals get the proteins, fats and carbohydrates they need by eating plants. These animals are called herbivores. Some animals catch and eat other animals. These meat eaters are called carnivores. Carnivores have special features to help them catch and kill other animals. These features may include sharp eyes that look to the front to help them see their prey.

Science quiz

The animals below are all carnivores. Draw a ring around the parts of each animal that help it catch and kill its prey.

Hawk

Pike

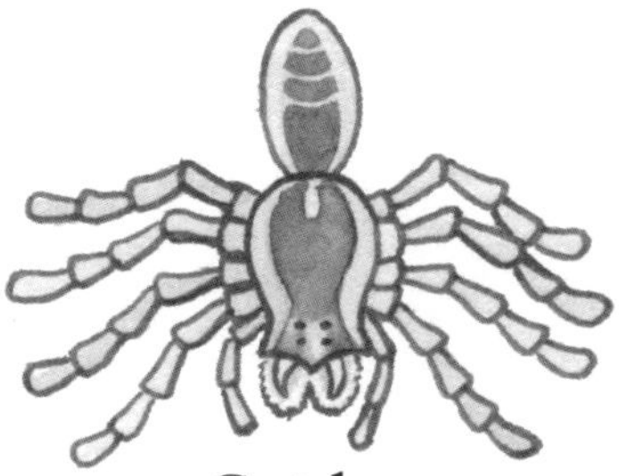

Spider

Lobster

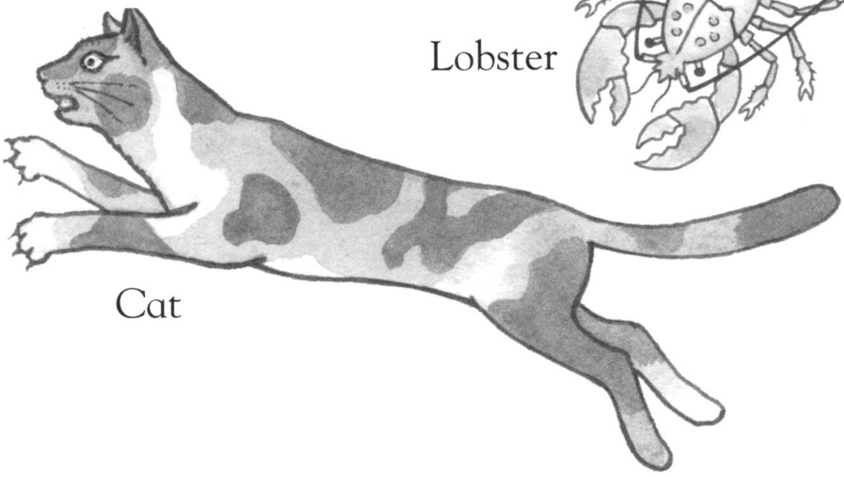

Cat

Science activity

Use a shallow dish to make a bird table. Make sure the dish is off the ground to protect the birds from cats. Put seeds on the table one day and mealworms on it the next. Write down which birds are herbivores and which birds are carnivores.

What is a human skeleton?

Science facts

The human skeleton has about 206 bones. It supports and shapes the body and protects the soft internal organs.

Science quiz

Look at the picture and use the words in the box to complete the sentences.

Backbone	Elbow	Pelvis	Rib cage	Skull	Femur

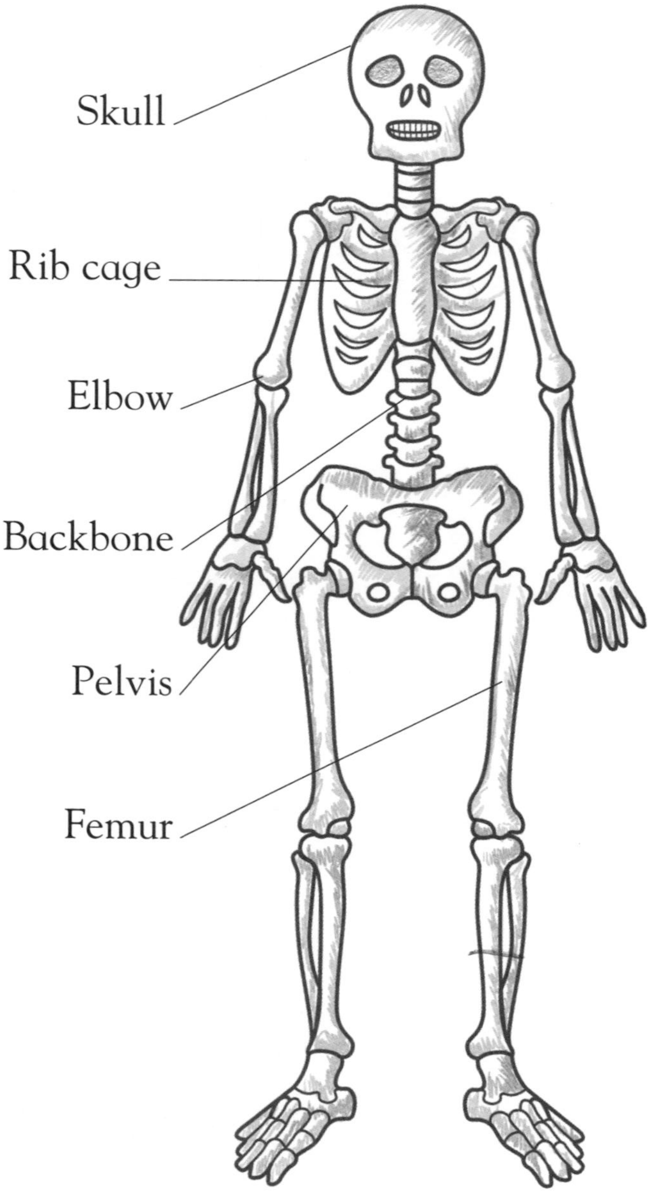

1 The bones of the upper arm and forearm meet at a joint called the Elbow.

2 The Rib cage protects the heart and lungs.

3 The SKull protects the brain.

4 The BacKBone protects the spinal cord.

5 The Pelvis protects some of the digestive and reproductive organs.

6 The Femur is the longest single bone in the body.

Do all animals have bones?

Science facts

Animals with bony skeletons inside them are called vertebrates. All vertebrates have a backbone. Vertebrates include humans, dogs, snakes, fish and birds. Skeletons give protection and support to the body and help it move. Animals, such as worms, insects, snails and jellyfish do not have bony skeletons; they are called invertebrates.

Science quiz

Here are the skeletons of a fish, a bird and a frog. On each of the drawings, colour in the part that protects the brain and colour in the backbone.

Fish

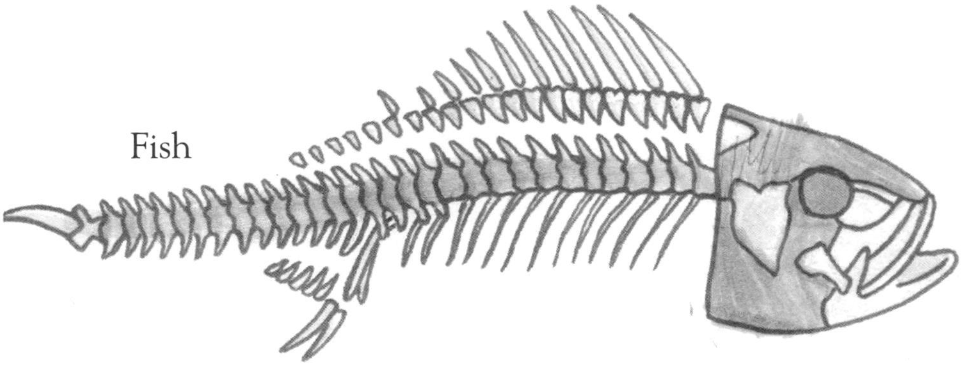

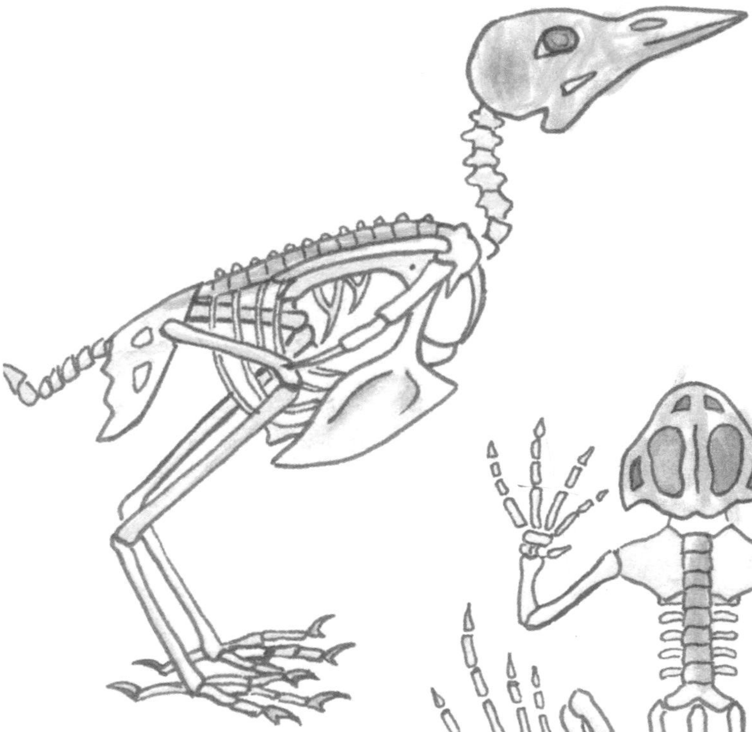

Bird

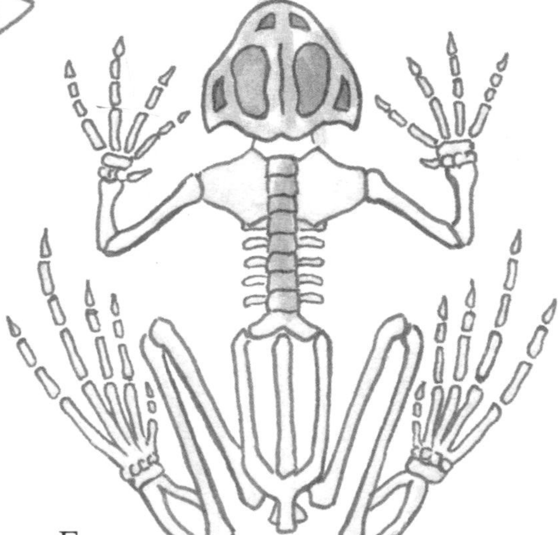

Frog

Science activity

(!) How strong are chicken bones? Next time you eat chicken, save as many bones as you can. (If you are a vegetarian, ask a friend to save you some.) How easy is it to break a leg bone? Are all the bones very hard? Can you find the joints in a wing?

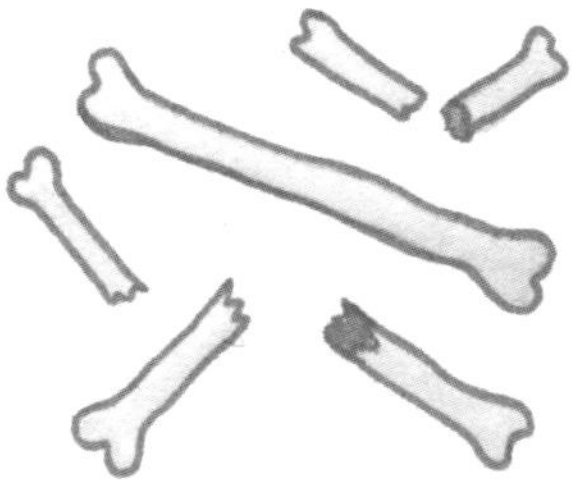

Where are your muscles?

Science facts

When muscles work, they get thicker and shorter. We say that the muscles contract. A contracting muscle pulls on a bone, making it move. There are muscles all over your body. Muscles need sugar and oxygen to work. They get both of these things from the blood. Most muscles rest after they have been used, but the heart muscle works non-stop throughout your life.

Science quiz

When you move your legs, feet, hands or arms, the muscles that move them get thicker and shorter.

On picture A, draw an arrow pointing to where you think the muscles moving the foot will get thicker.

On picture B, draw an arrow pointing to where you think the muscle raising the forearm will get thicker.

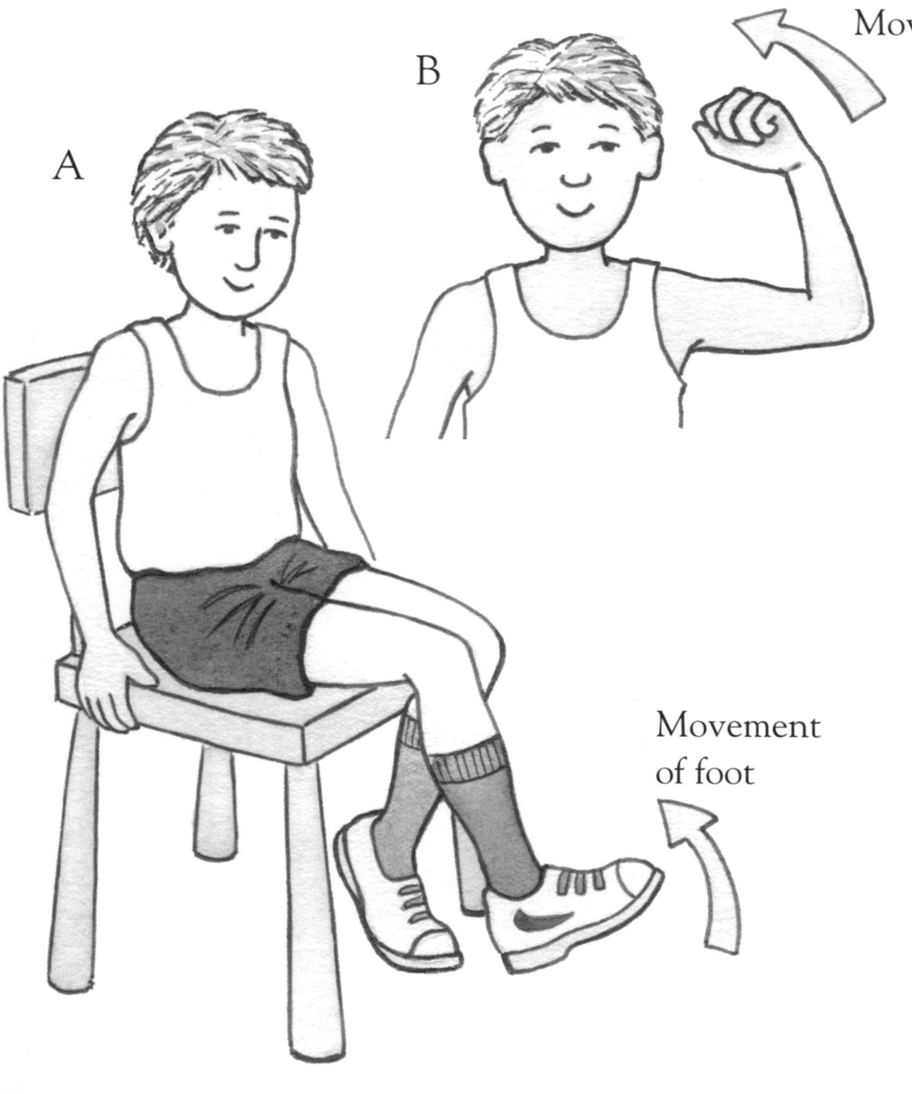

Science activity

Put both hands around the top of your leg. Lift the lower part of your leg by straightening your knee. Which muscles thicken and shorten as your lower leg moves?

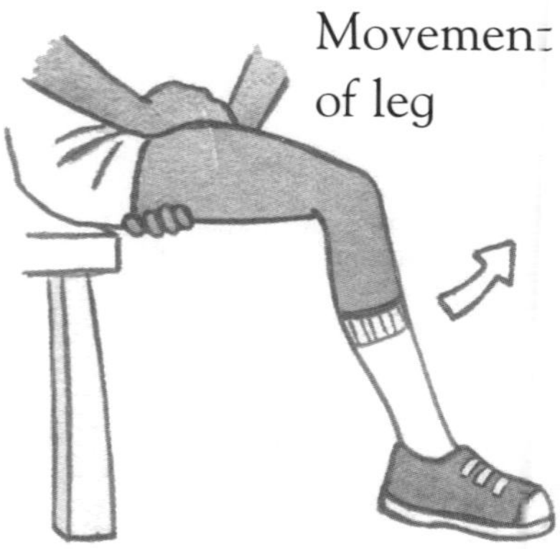

Is it a rock?

Science facts

Mountains, hills, cliffs, stones and pebbles are made of rock. Jewels are made of rock. Garden soil and sand are made up of many tiny bits of rock. There are many different types of rock. Some rocks are very hard; others are soft.

Science quiz

Colour all the different rocks you can see in this picture.

Science activity

Start a rock collection. But remember to ask an adult before you take any rocks from a beach or park. Are all your rocks the same colour?

What sort of rock is it?

Science facts

Rocks are very hard materials. Some rocks, called ores, contain metals. Others contain fossils of animals or plants that died millions of years ago. Many rocks contain crystals. A few rock crystals, such as diamond, are extremely valuable because they are very rare. These crystals are called gems. Some rocks, such as sandstone, are made when mud or grains of sand are slowly squashed together.

Science quiz

Use this Yes/No key to find the names of the rocks in the pictures.

Clue 1 Are there fossils in the rock? If yes, it is limestone.
If there are no fossils to be seen, go to clue 2.

Clue 2 If there are crystals in the rock, go to clue 3.
If there are no crystals in the rock, it is sandstone.

Clue 3 Are the crystals big? If yes, it is calcite.
Are the crystals small? If yes, it is granite.

A ....

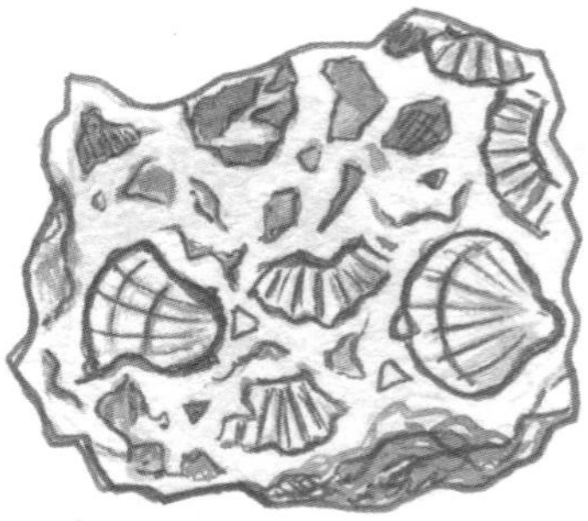

C ....

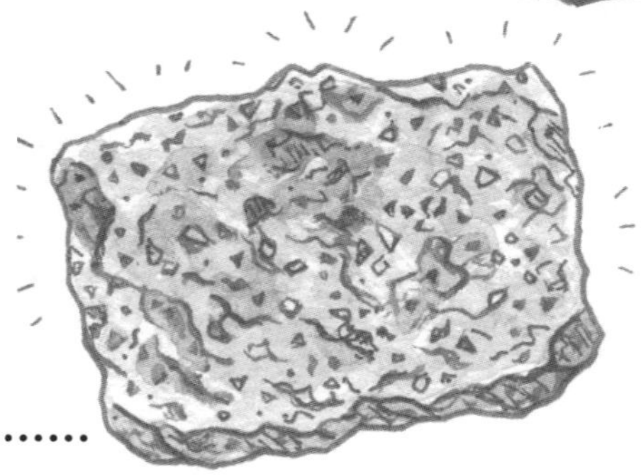

B ....

D ....

Science activity

Look in the window of a local jewellery shop. How many different gems can you see? Which gems are the brightest? Which gems are the most expensive?

Do rocks absorb water?

Science facts

Different types of rock are formed in different ways. Each type of rock has a different set of properties. One property of a rock is its porosity. This is the ability of the rock to absorb water. Water is held in rocks under the ground. The more porous the rock, the more water it can hold.

Science quiz

Some rocks were weighed. They were placed in water for an hour and then weighed again.

Rock	Weight before	Weight after
Granite	100 N	101 N
Chalk	50 N	100 N
Sandstone	100 N	150 N
Marble	75 N	76 N

Which rock absorbed the most water for its weight?

....

What sorts of plant do you think will grow in areas where granite is the underlying rock? Use the chart above to help you answer this question.

....

....

Science activity

You can check the porosity of materials in a different way. Collect two different types of brick. Place each one in a bowl of shallow water and leave them for 30 minutes. Take them out and compare them by looking at how far the water has crept up each brick. Is one brick more porous than the other?

Which rock is this?

Science facts

There are many different types of rock. Some common rocks are granite, chalk, sandstone, limestone, flint and slate. They differ in the way they look and in their properties. Scientists often use keys to help identify rocks.

Science quiz

Use the Yes/No key below to identify these two rocks.

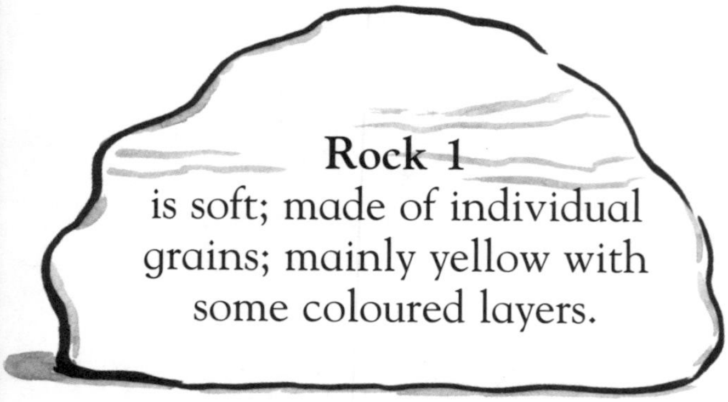
Rock 1
is soft; made of individual grains; mainly yellow with some coloured layers.

....

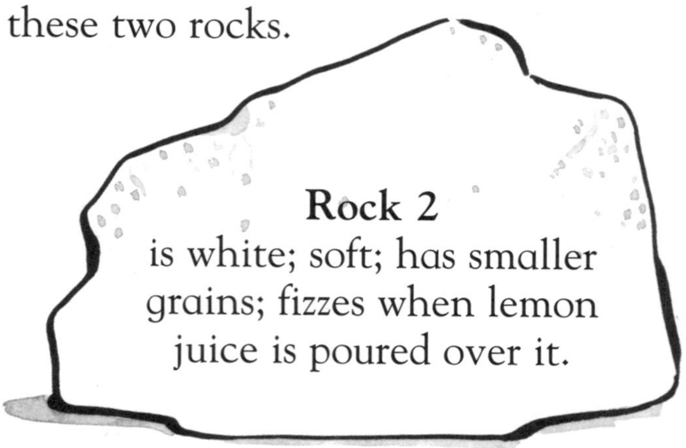
Rock 2
is white; soft; has smaller grains; fizzes when lemon juice is poured over it.

....

Key to some common rocks
1 Does the rock fizz when lemon juice is poured over it? If yes, go to 2; if no, go to 4. 2 Is the rock hard? If yes, it is limestone; if no, then go to 3. 3 The rock is chalk. 4 Does the rock have layers? If yes, go to 7; if no, go to 5. 5 Does the rock contain crystals? If yes, it is granite; if no, go to 6. 6 The rock is flint. 7 Is the rock soft and made of individual grains? If yes, it is sandstone; if no, go to 8. 8 The rock is slate.

Science activity

Keys help to identify things. Different keys help scientists identify different things, such as types of grass, insect or wild flower. How good are you at making keys? Collect some objects from home and make up a key to identify them. Try out your key on someone else. Does it work?

What is in the soil?

Science facts

Soil is made up mainly of small pieces, or particles, of rock. Tiny rock particles form mud when you add water to the soil. Soil can also contain slightly larger rock particles, such as sand grains. Heavier pieces of rock are called stones. Soil also contains humus (mainly rotted plant material).

Science quiz

Hannah dug some soil from her garden and put it into a plastic bottle with some water. She shook the bottle very hard until it was a muddy mixture, as shown in picture A. She left it for one hour and then came back to look at it again. Picture B shows what she saw.

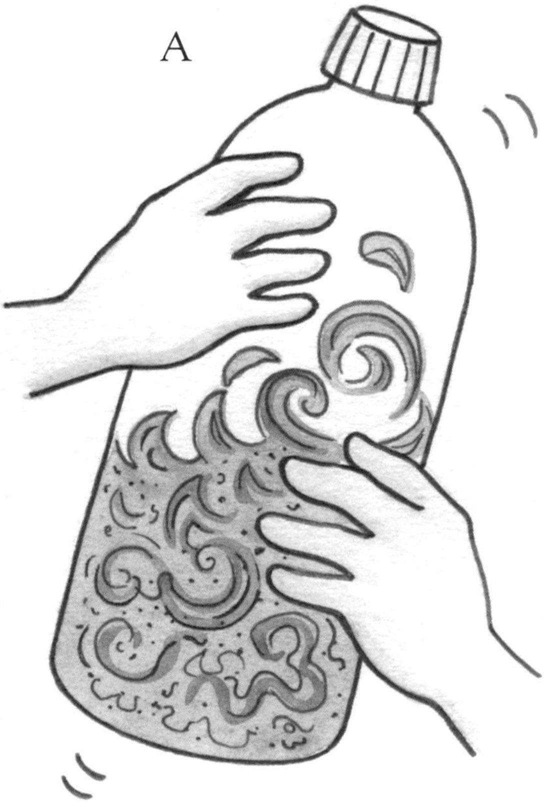

Bottle of shaken mud and water

Bottle after being left to stand for 1 hour

Can you explain what happened?

....

....

Science activity

(!) Look at soil with a magnifying glass. Can you see the different-sized particles? Is there any dead plant matter in the soil? Are there any tiny creatures in it? (Always wear gloves when handling soil.)

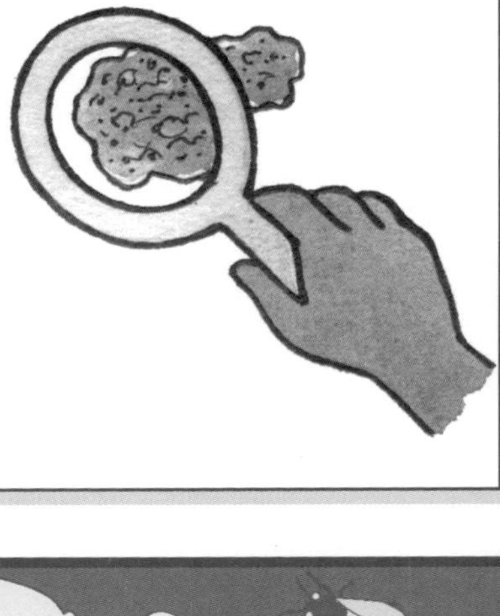

Which soil holds water best?

Science facts

Different types of soil contain different sizes of rock particle. Soil with very fine particles is called silt or clay. Sandy soils contain slightly larger particles. Other soils contain lots of stones. Most soil is a mixture of all of these different-sized particles. The more sand and stones the soil contains, the easier it is for water to pass through the soil.

Science quiz

A class set up an experiment to find out which type of soil let the most water pass through it. One bottle held sandy soil, one held silt and clay, and one held a mixture of silt, clay and sand. The same amount of water was poured into each bottle. Holes in the bottom of each bottle let water passing through the soil drain into a beaker underneath. This is how they looked after 30 minutes.

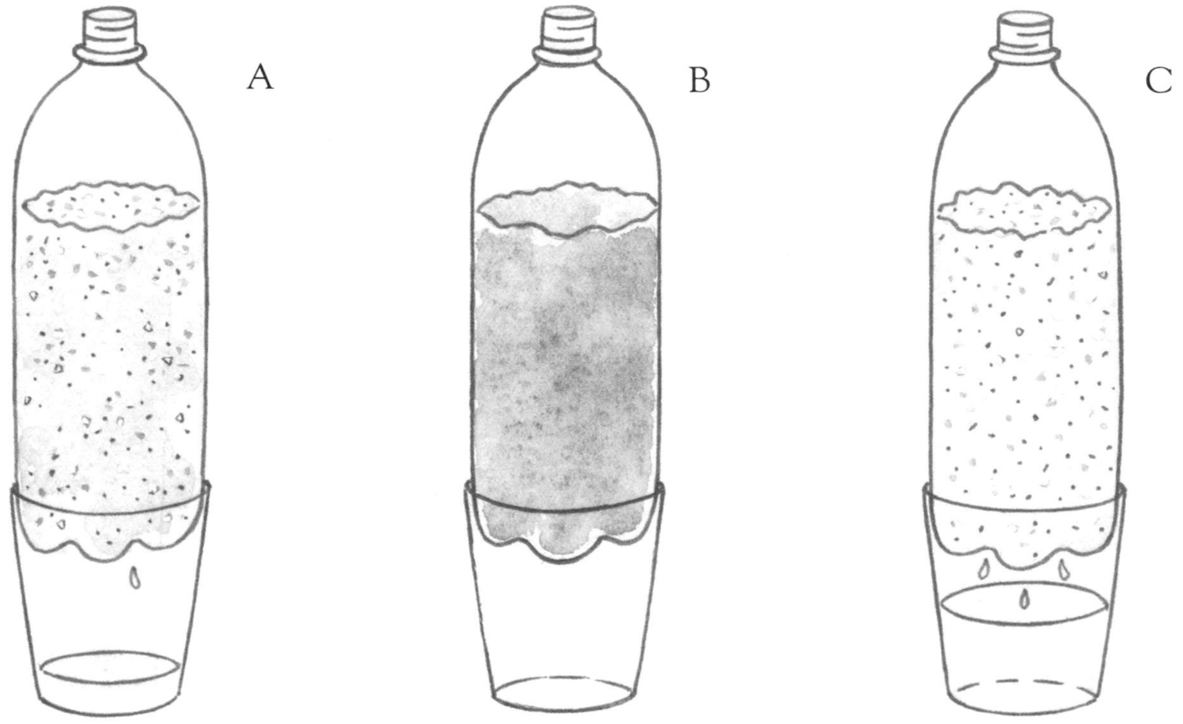

Which bottle contained the sandy soil? ....

Science activity

(!) Try growing mung beans in a pot of garden soil. Do the same in pots of peat, compost and bulb fibre. In which material do the beans grow best? (Always wear gloves when handling garden soil.)

What kind of soil is this?

Science facts

Soil is made up of grains of broken rock and humus (mainly rotted plant material). A soil's type depends on the mix of humus and on the size of the grains of rock. The grains can be very small and smooth, such as in clay, or they can be larger, like grains of sand, pieces of gravel, or stones.

Science quiz

Use this key to identify the soil described below.

The soil is light in colour, gritty and drains well. The soil is ....

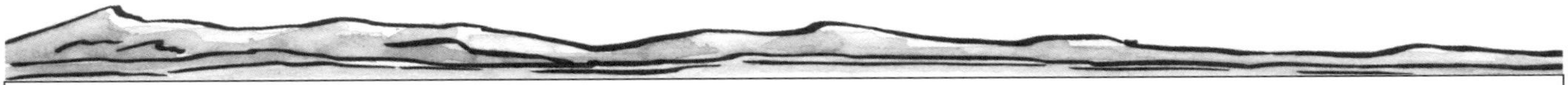

Does the soil feel gritty?

- Yes → Is the soil light in colour and does it drain very quickly?
  - Yes → Sandy
  - No → Loam
- No → Does the soil have very small grains and does it hold water?
  - Yes → Clay
  - No → Peat

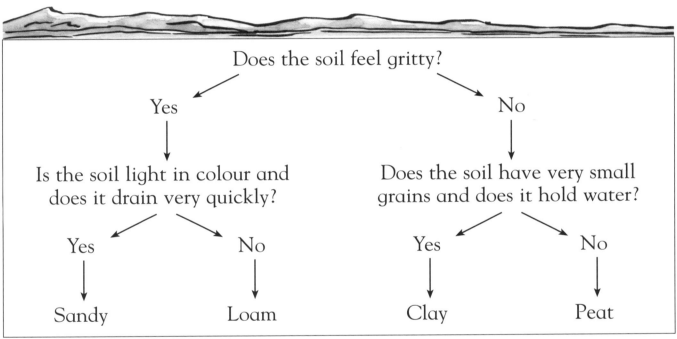

Different plants prefer different types of soil. If a plant had roots that could rot very easily in water, which type of soil might help it grow well?

....

....

Science activity

(!) You can see the different parts that make up a soil by using water to separate them. Pour water into an empty jar until it is three-quarters full. Stir in three or four dessertspoons of soil and mix well. Allow time for the soil to settle so you can see the different parts. Try different soils. What do they look like?

Where does light come from?

Science facts

The light that we see with our eyes comes from objects called light sources. Light sources include the Sun, flames from candles and fires, and electric lamps. A few animals, such as fireflies, are light sources because they can make light inside their bodies. Light always travels in a straight line from a light source to our eyes. (Never look directly at the Sun, because its bright light can damage your eyes.)

Science quiz

The picture on the right shows how light from a fluorescent lamp reaches the eyes of the boy. Draw arrows to show how the light reaches the eyes of the children in the pictures below.

Fluorescent lamp

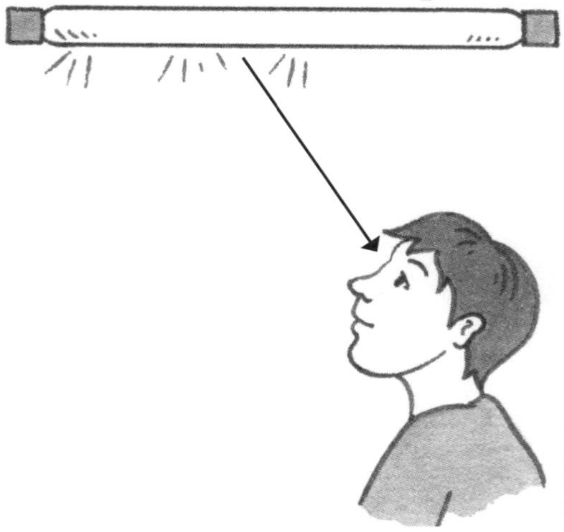

Science activity

(!) Try draping a duvet or some blankets over chairs and other furniture to make a very dark place where no light can get in. Take a torch into your dark place. This is your light source.

Can you see through it?

Science facts

Materials that you can see clearly through, such as glass, are said to be transparent. Opaque materials, such as rock, are those that you cannot see through at all. You cannot see clearly through translucent materials, but if you hold a torch behind them you can see a bright patch of light.

Science quiz

Can you fill in the missing words in this table?

Material	Can you see through it?	Can you see torch light through it?	Scientific description
Aluminium kitchen foil	No	....	Opaque
Kitchen clingfilm	Yes	Yes	....
Greaseproof paper	No	Yes	....
Tissue paper	....	....	Translucent
Cardboard	No	No	....
Cotton handkerchief	....	....	Translucent

Science activity

(!) Ask an adult to boil some water for you. Let the water cool and then use some of it to cover the bottom of a plastic container. In another plastic container, cover the bottom with tap water. Place both containers in a freezer and check them two or three hours later. Does the ice in the containers look different, and if so why?

Where is the shadow?

Science facts

You cannot see through objects that are opaque because light will not pass through them. When you put an opaque object between a light source and a wall, a dark area called a shadow forms on the wall. The shadow forms because the object stops light from reaching the wall. Remember that light always travels in straight lines.

Science quiz

Mina taped a cardboard circle to a drinking straw. Then she held the circle in front of a shining torch, so that a shadow formed on the wall. Can you draw the shadow that formed on the wall?

Science activity

Use a torch to form a shadow of an object on a wall. What happens to the shadow when you move the torch nearer to the object? What happens to the shadow when you move the object closer to the wall?

What makes things shiny?

Science facts

Shiny objects have very smooth surfaces, which reflect light especially well. These objects reflect a lot of light into our eyes, making them appear shiny.

Science quiz

The picture on the right shows how light reflects off a shiny ring and into the girl's eyes. Use a ruler to draw arrows that show how the light reflects off these shiny things into the eyes of the children.

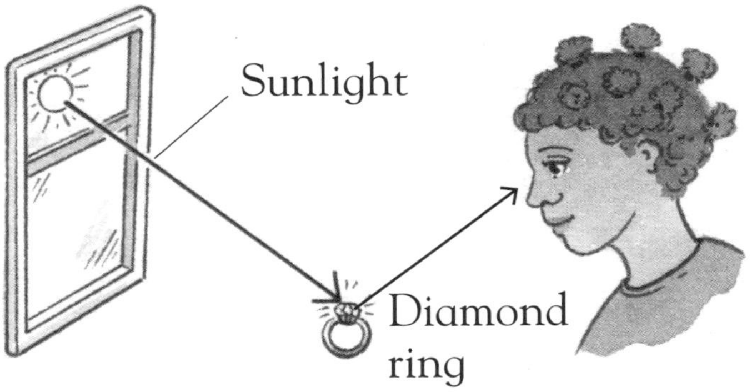

Science activity

If you look into the hollow of a shiny spoon, what does your reflection look like? Turn the spoon over and look into the underside of the spoon. Now what does your reflection look like?

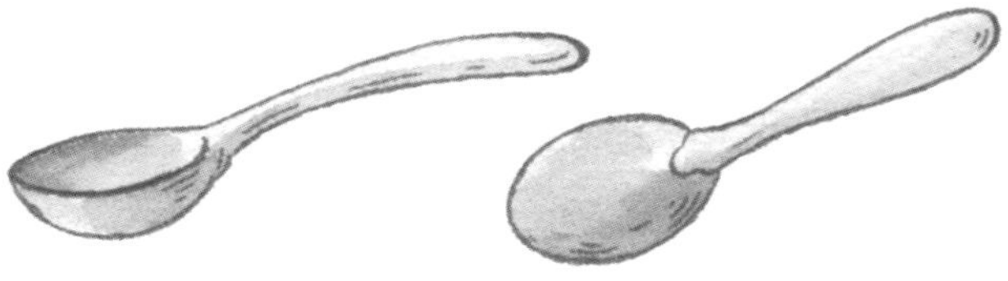

Is it a push or a pull?

Science facts

Forces can make things move. Pushes and pulls are examples of forces that make things move. Magnets push and pull each other because they have a force called magnetism. The Earth pulls things downwards with a force called gravity. Squashes are pushes that make objects change shape.

Science quiz

The pictures show a number of forces in action. Decide whether each force is a push, a pull or a squash. Write your answer beside each picture.

This force is a ....

This force is a ....

This force is a ....

This force is a ....

This force is a ....

This force is a ....

Science activity

Try pushing against bathroom scales. The scales will show you how hard you are pushing. Can you push harder with your hand or your finger? Does a leg push harder than an arm? Who is the best pusher in your family?

Is the surface rough or smooth?

Science facts

When you kick a ball, it starts moving then gradually slows down until it stops. The force that makes the ball slow down is called friction. Friction is a force between two surfaces that are touching, such as the surface of a ball and the ground. Rough surfaces produce more friction than smooth ones.

Science quiz

Mary and Sean rolled marbles down a tube and measured how far each marble rolled. They tried rolling the marbles over different surfaces. They kept the angle of the tube the same each time. Here are their results.

Surface	Distance marble rolls
Gravel path	21 cm
Grass	3 cm
Kitchen floor	163 cm
Carpet	32 cm
Pavement	85 cm

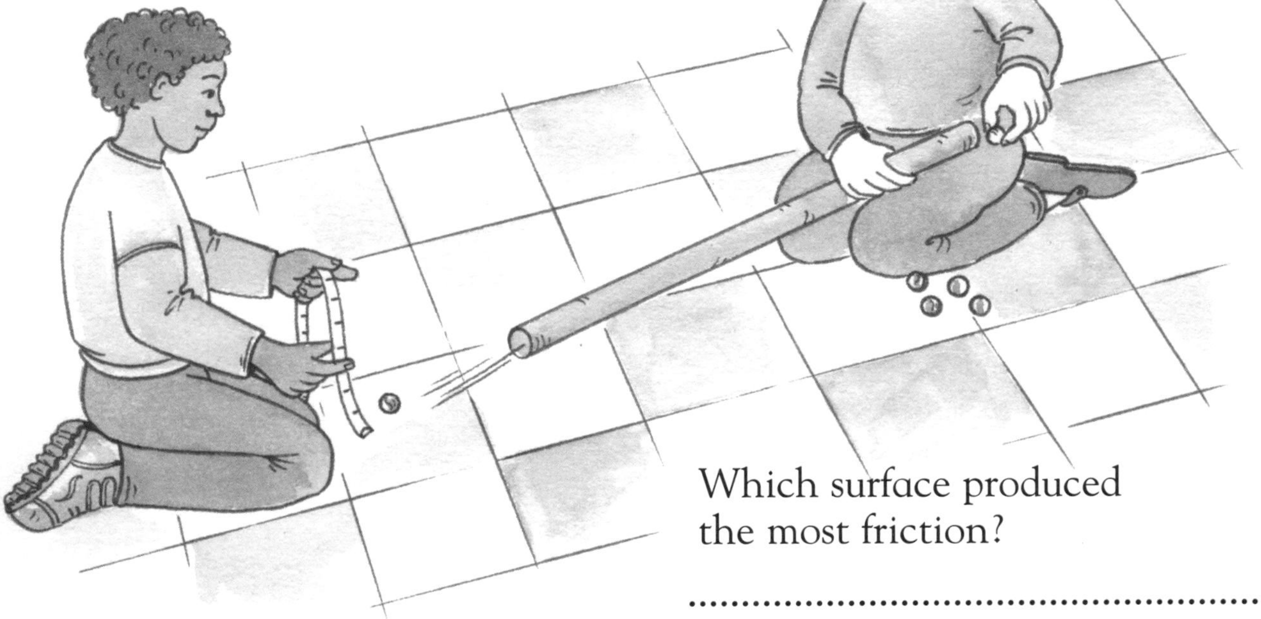

Which surface produced the most friction?

....

Science activity

Slide coins down a slightly tilted table top or wooden board. Wet the surface a little and try sliding the coins down it again. Is a dry or wet surface best for sliding? Which surface produces the most friction?

Is it attracted to a magnet?

Science facts

A magnet will try to pull some metal objects towards itself. We say that the magnet attracts these objects. Magnets will attract only objects containing the metals iron, steel, cobalt or nickel. They will not attract other metals.

Science quiz

Draw a line from the magnet to each of the metal objects it will attract.

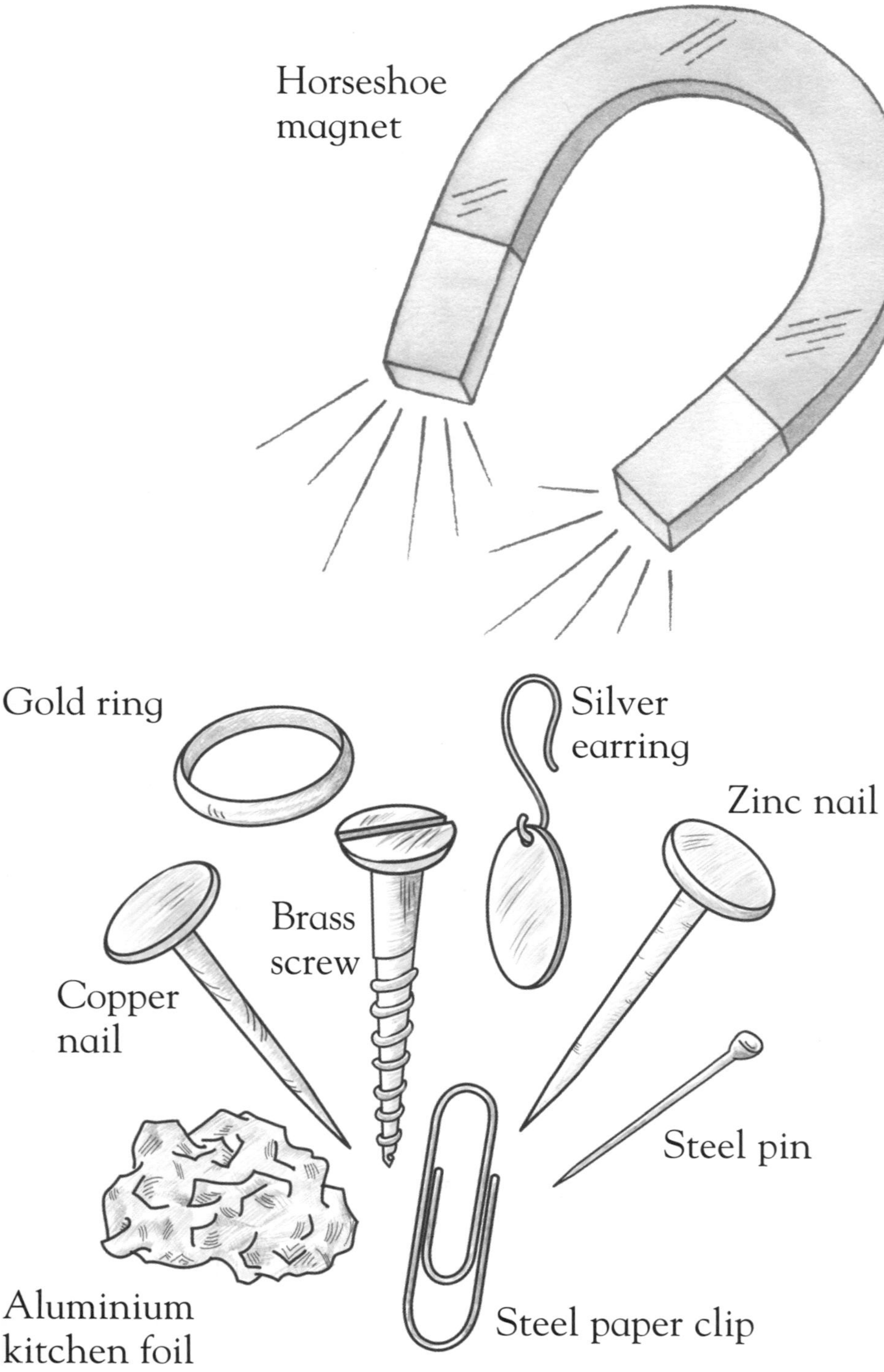

Science activity

Will a magnet attract things through a sheet of paper? Will it attract through two sheets? What about ten sheets? Try attracting things through other materials, such as plastic or cloth.

Which is the best magnet?

Science facts

The most common magnets we see are those that stick to refrigerator doors. Magnets can be many different shapes and sizes. Some are horseshoe shaped. Others are shaped like rings, bars, discs and rods. Some magnets are very strong and attract things from a long way away.

Science quiz

Each of these magnets was dipped into a box of steel paper clips. Put a tick (✔) below the strongest magnet.

Science activity

Stroke a metal coat hanger repeatedly with the end of a bar magnet. Always stroke in the same direction and lift the magnet away from the coat hanger between strokes. You will find that the coat hanger becomes a magnet, too. Will the coat hanger pick up as many steel paper clips as the bar magnet?

Do they attract or repel?

Science facts

On every magnet, there are two areas where the magnetism is strongest. These areas are called the magnet's north and south poles. A north pole of one magnet will always attract the south pole of another magnet. However, if two north poles or two south poles are placed together, they will push each other apart. These magnets repel each other.

Science quiz

Look at the pairs of magnets shown in the pictures. Which pairs will attract each other? Which pairs will repel each other? Circle the right answers.

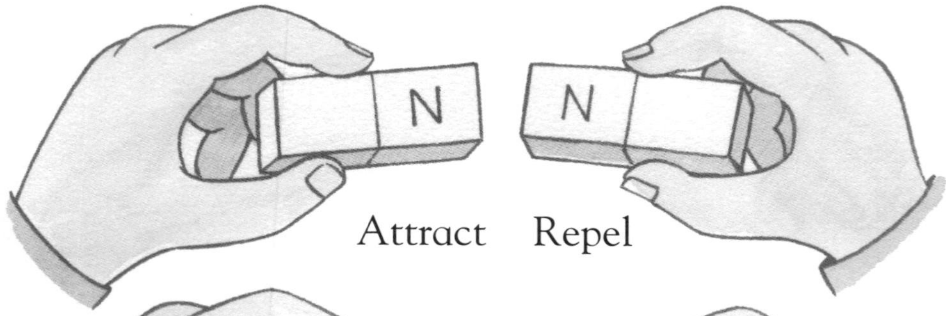

Attract Repel

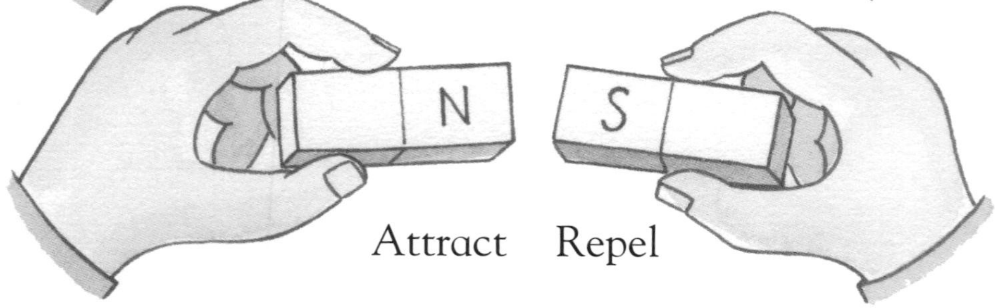

Attract Repel

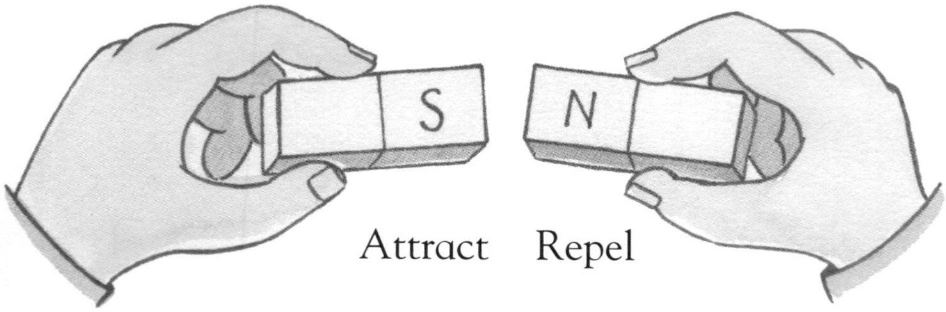

Attract Repel

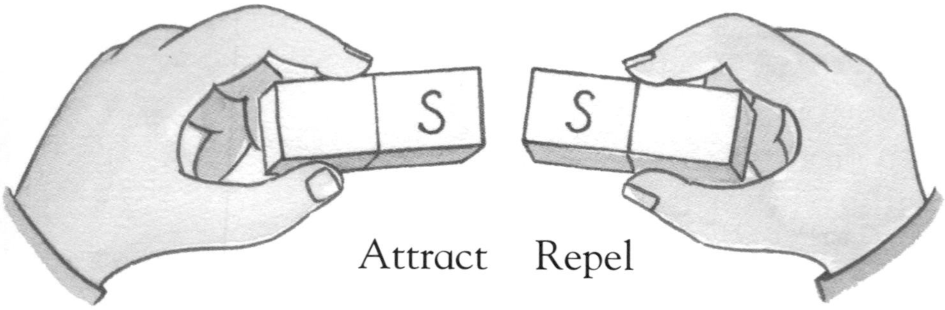

Attract Repel

Science activity

How could you stack a pile of bar magnets? Make a drawing of the pile, marking the north poles with the letter **N** and the south poles with the letter **S**.

Answer Section with Parents' Notes

Key Stage 2 Ages 7–8

This section provides answers and explanatory notes to the quizzes and activities in the book. Work through each page together and ensure that your child understands each task. Point out any mistakes in your child's work and correct any errors, but also remember to praise your child's efforts and achievements. Where appropriate, ask your child to predict the outcome of the *Science activity* experiments. After each experiment, challenge your child to explain the results.

(!) If a *Science activity* box includes this caution symbol, extra care is necessary. In such cases, experiments may involve heavy weights, sharp objects, hot water, ice or soil. Always wear gloves when handling soil and ensure hands are washed afterwards. Gloves are also advisable for activities in which hot or very cold objects are used.

2

Is it alive?

Science facts
All living things have seven processes in common. Every living thing can **M**ove, **R**eproduce, and is **S**ensitive to the world around it. Each one can also **G**row, **R**espire (use the gases in air), **E**xcrete (get rid of waste from its body) and use food by a process called **N**utrition. To help you remember the processes, put the first letter of each one together to spell **MRS GREN**.

Science quiz
The words below describe the seven life processes of living things. Draw a line from each word to the picture that shows it happening.

Science activity

Which is the most sensitive part of your body? Collect some objects, such as coins, toys or vegetables. With your eyes shut, can you tell which object is which using your toes? How well can you feel the objects with your elbows?

Although the curriculum only requires knowledge of nutrition, movement, reproduction and growth, it is useful to point out the other features when you see them, such as a cat breathing, a seagull excreting or a woodlouse's sensitivity to light.

3

Are plants alive?

Science facts
Plants are living things, but they are different from animals. Plants make their own food inside their leaves. They make the food using sunlight, gas from the air, and water from the soil. They use this food to grow. Plants can reproduce to make new plants. Unlike animals, plants do not move from place to place, but they are sensitive to light and always grow towards it.

Science quiz
Here are some facts about an oak tree. Put a tick (✔) beside any fact that tells you the oak tree is alive.

- [x] The leaves of the tree make food.
- [ ] Birds nest in the branches.
- [x] It takes in water through its roots.
- [ ] The branches move in the wind.
- [x] It produces acorns in autumn.
- [ ] Squirrels eat the acorns.
- [x] It grows 300 mm each year.

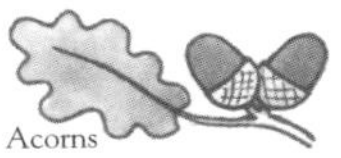

Science activity

(!) Put a few acorns or seeds in a flowerpot with some soil or compost. Water them regularly. Make sure they get plenty of light. Eventually, each one may sprout a shoot. What happens if you keep on watering the shoots? How can you tell if they are alive?

Trees and plants cannot move around, so children find it hard to understand that they are living things. They can understand that green leaves are a sign of life. This is harder to grasp in winter, when some lose their leaves and, to a child, may seem lifeless.

4

How do plants stay healthy?

Science facts
Plants make their own food. They take gas from the air and water from the soil to make sugar and starch. Chlorophyll allows plants to absorb sunlight, gives plants their green colour, and helps them make their food. A plant's roots take water from the soil. There are special minerals in the water that help the plant grow and stay healthy.

Science quiz
Andrew wanted to find out the best way to grow cress. He took three dishes, put cotton wool in each one and sprinkled cress seeds over the cotton wool. He put dishes **A** and **B** on a window ledge and dish **C** in a dark cupboard. He watered dishes **A** and **C** every day, but not dish **B**. This is how the dishes looked after two weeks. Label each dish **A**, **B** or **C** to show which is which.

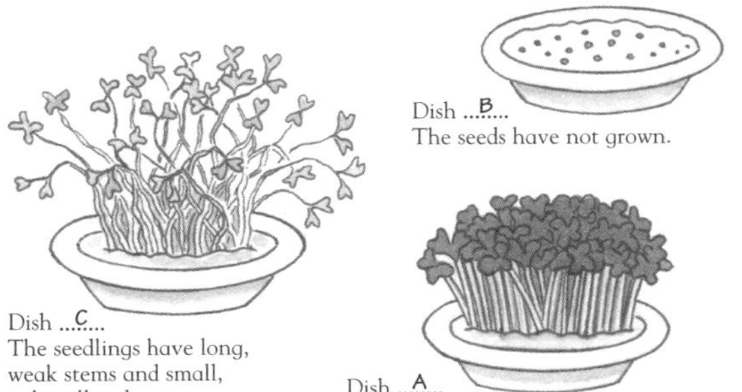

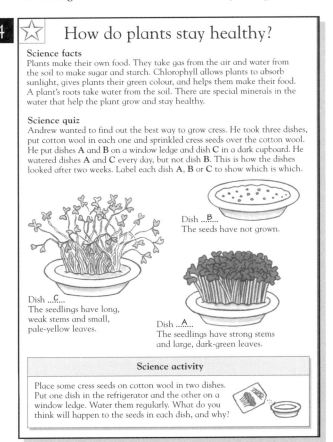

Dish ...B...
The seeds have not grown.

Dish ...C...
The seedlings have long, weak stems and small, pale-yellow leaves.

Dish ...A...
The seedlings have strong stems and large, dark-green leaves.

Science activity

Place some cress seeds on cotton wool in two dishes. Put one dish in the refrigerator and the other on a window ledge. Water them regularly. What do you think will happen to the seeds in each dish, and why?

All seeds need water to germinate. Seedlings kept in the dark grow quickly to try to find the light. They cannot absorb light to make food, so they will have yellow leaves. Their stems will be weak. Cress seeds sprout very slowly in cold places.

5 Are all roots the same?

Science facts
Plants use their roots to hold themselves in the soil. The other main job of a root is to take in water from the soil. The plant uses the water to make its food. Some roots go down a long way into the soil to find water. Other roots spread out widely to use water all around them. The roots of some plants become very fat because the plant stores food in them.

Science quiz
Mina likes helping her mother in the garden. One of her favourite jobs is pulling up weeds. Here are some weeds that she found.

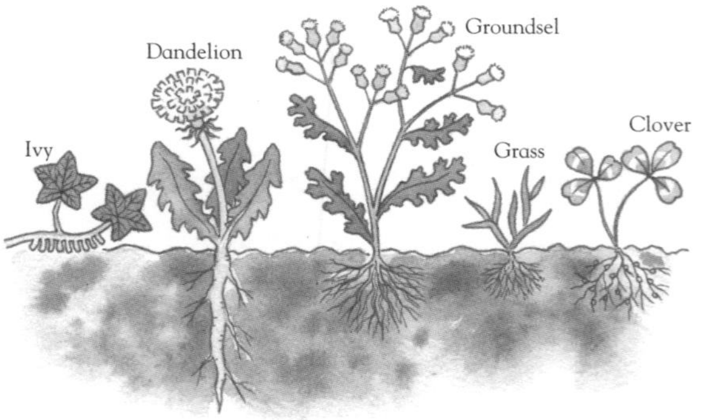

Why is dandelion the hardest to pull up? It has a very long, fat root.

Why is ivy the easiest to pull up? It has very short roots.

Science activity

Some of the vegetables that we eat are swollen plant roots. How many different root vegetables can you find in your local greengrocer's or supermarket?

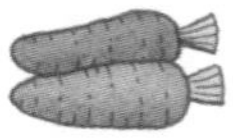

Generally, the longer a plant's roots, the harder it is to pull the plant from the ground. When gardening, ask your child to place weeds in order of how hard/easy they are to pull up. Carrot, turnip, parsnip and radish are all examples of swollen roots.

6 Are all leaves the same?

Science facts
Leaves are usually green because they have a green chemical inside them called chlorophyll, which catches sunlight. They also have tiny holes on their surface to let air and water in and out. Leaves use sunlight, air and water to make food.

Science quiz
Use this branching Yes/No key to find out what tree each leaf comes from.

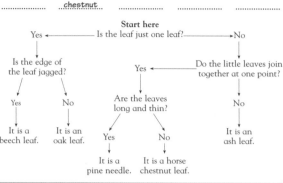

A Beech   B Horse chestnut   C Oak   D Ash   E Pine

Start here

Is the leaf just one leaf?
- Yes → Is the edge of the leaf jagged?
  - Yes → It is a beech leaf.
  - No → It is an oak leaf.
- No → Do the little leaves join together at one point?
  - Yes → Are the leaves long and thin?
    - Yes → It is a pine needle.
    - No → It is a horse chestnut leaf.
  - No → It is an ash leaf.

Science activity

(!) Make a collection of leaves from your garden or local park. Can you sort the leaves into different groups? What features do the leaves in each group have in common?

Leaves are designed to capture as much light as possible for a tree. They grow on the tree in such a way as to fill every gap where light shines between the branches. To make this clearer, get your child to stand under a tree and look upwards.

7 What do plants do with water?

Science facts
All plants have roots that perform two functions. Firstly, they anchor the plant to the ground. Secondly, they absorb water from the soil. Dissolved chemicals in the water, called nutrients, are needed for healthy plant growth. Plants also need water to make their food. Water is carried from the roots, through thin tubes in the stems, to every part of the plant. When the water reaches the surface of the leaves, it evaporates, causing more water to travel up the stem.

A small plastic bag tied around the leaf of a plant shows how water evaporates from the leaves. After a few hours in a sunny place, tiny water droplets form on the inside of the bag.

Science quiz
Gordon cut all the roots off a broad-bean plant and planted it in a flowerpot. He continued to water the plant, but after two days it started to wilt and after four days it was dead. Explain why this happened.

Though water was available in the soil, the plant died because it was unable to absorb the water without its roots.

Science activity

(!) Take two stalks of celery with a small amount of root. Remove the leaves from one stalk. Put the stalks in coloured water (use food colouring) and leave them for two days. Ask an adult to help you slice through one of the stalks about 3 cm from the bottom. Draw a picture of the pattern that you see. How far has the coloured water travelled up each stalk? Is there a difference? Why?

Roots not only anchor plants in the ground but also absorb water, which is transported to all parts of the plant through vessels in the stem. The water travels up farther in the stalk with leaves, showing that leaves assist water uptake.

8 Do all plants have flowers?

Science facts
Most plants produce seeds that grow into new plants. The seeds of conifer trees grow inside woody cones. The seeds of other plants grow inside flowers. Ferns and mosses have neither cones nor flowers. Instead, they have special parts that produce tiny specks called spores, which grow into new plants.

Science quiz
Some of the plants in the pictures below are flowering plants. Circle the flowers.

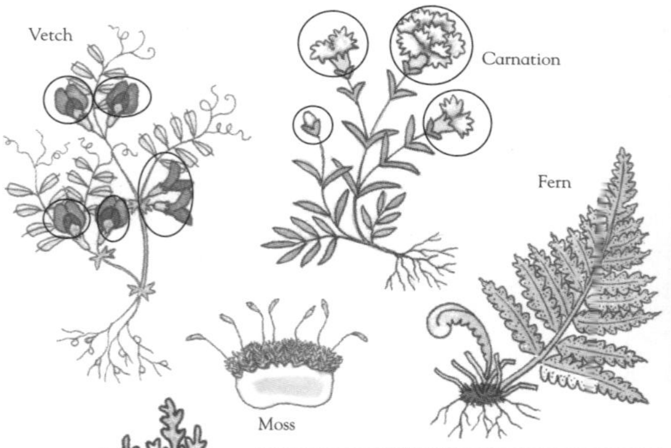

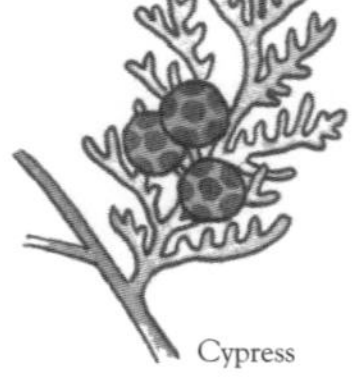

Science activity

How many different kinds of flower are there in your local flower shop? Visit a garden centre or plant nursery to find examples of non-flowering plants, such as ferns and conifers.

Your child will learn that plants can be grouped according to their features. The main groups are flowering plants, cone-bearing conifers and spore-producing horsetails, ferns, mosses and clubmosses. Fungi produce spores, but they are not true plants.

9 What kind of seed is it?

Science facts
Seeds germinate (sprout) to grow into new plants. Many seeds grow inside flowers. Fruits then form around some seeds to protect them. There are many different kinds of fruit, some of which we eat. We eat nuts as well, which are seeds with a hard, woody shell. Some children are allergic to nuts. If they eat nuts they get very sick. Always ask an adult before you eat nuts.

Science quiz
Which seed comes from which fruit? Draw a line from each fruit to its seed.

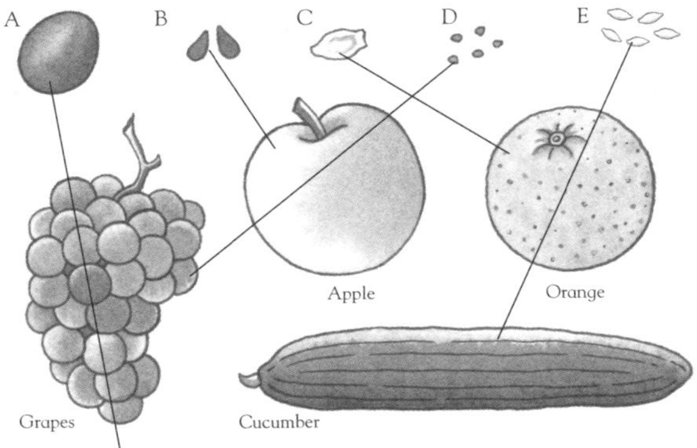

Science activity

(!) How many different kinds of seed are there in a packet of birdseed? Sort them into groups. What is different about each group? Which seeds do birds prefer?

Draw your child's attention to seeds in fruits and salads eaten at mealtimes. Children will also be interested to find out which grain seed is used to make their favourite breakfast cereal – is it wheat, barley, oats, rice or a mixture of seeds?

10 How do seeds grow in new places?

Science facts
A plant produces many seeds. If all the seeds fell to the ground around a parent plant, they would choke each other when they started to grow. Seeds are adapted so that they can be dispersed as widely as possible. Some are suited to being dispersed by the wind and others by water. Seeds inside juicy fruits are dispersed after being eaten by birds and other animals.

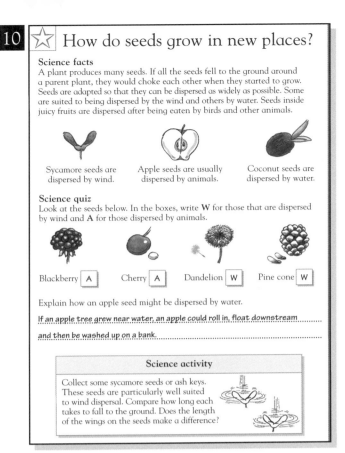

Sycamore seeds are dispersed by wind.

Apple seeds are usually dispersed by animals.

Coconut seeds are dispersed by water.

Science quiz
Look at the seeds below. In the boxes, write **W** for those that are dispersed by wind and **A** for those dispersed by animals.

Blackberry [A]

Cherry [A]

Dandelion [W]

Pine cone [W]

Explain how an apple seed might be dispersed by water.

If an apple tree grew near water, an apple could roll in, float downstream and then be washed up on a bank.

Science activity

Collect some sycamore seeds or ash keys. These seeds are particularly well suited to wind dispersal. Compare how long each takes to fall to the ground. Does the length of the wings on the seeds make a difference?

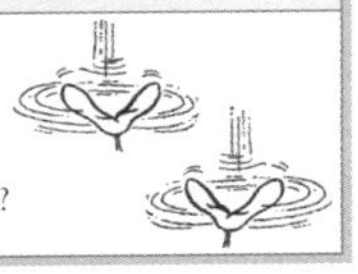

Encourage your child to predict what will happen to the winged seeds used in the *Science activity*. In general, the shorter the wing length, the quicker the seed falls to the ground because it encounters less air resistance.

11 What do seeds need to grow?

Science facts
Seeds need water to germinate and grow into new plants. Some seeds need to be kept in a warm place before they will start to grow, while others germinate best if they are kept cool.

Science quiz
Here are a number of beans that have been planted in different ways.

Bean A is planted in sand but not watered.

Bean B is planted in soil and watered every day.

Bean C is planted in soil but not watered.

Bean D is planted on cotton wool and watered every day.

Bean E has no soil or water.

Which beans do you think will grow?

Beans B and D

Why did you make this choice?

They are both watered every day.

Science activity

(!) A packet of birdseed contains many different types of seed. Plant each type in a different flowerpot. Put the same amount of soil in each pot and add a little water each day. Which type of seed germinates best?

As long as seeds have water, they will grow in many different materials, not just soil. In the birdseed activity, let your child decide what "germinates best" means: is it the first seed to sprout, the one that grows tallest or the one that grows leaves first?

12 Can food keep you healthy?

Science facts
Living things need food and water to stay alive. Foods such as milk, meat, fish, eggs and nuts contain proteins that help you grow. Other foods, such as fruit, bread and pasta, contain carbohydrates that give you energy to move and play. Fats, such as butter and margarine, also give you energy. Fruits and vegetables contain vitamins and minerals that keep you healthy.

Science quiz
Here are some of the foods that Jason found in his kitchen. He read the labels to find out which foods contain fats and which contain proteins.

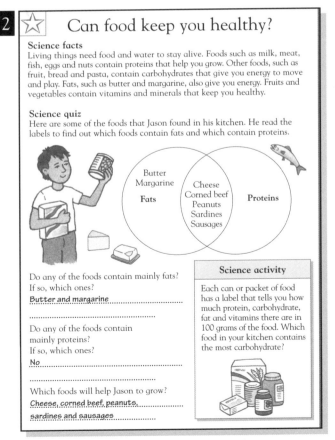

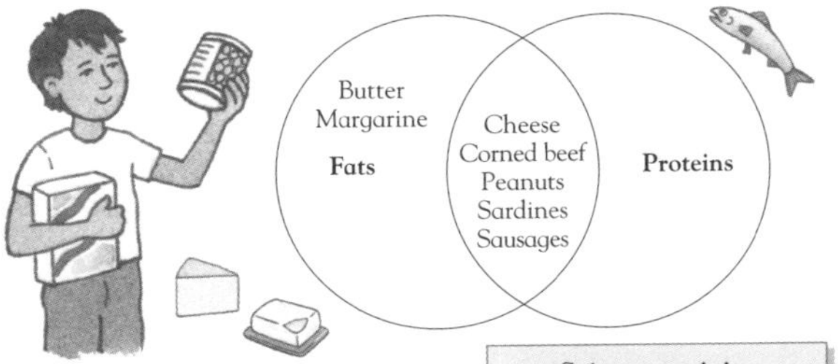

Do any of the foods contain mainly fats?
If so, which ones?

Butter and margarine

Do any of the foods contain mainly proteins?
If so, which ones?

No

Which foods will help Jason to grow?

Cheese, corned beef, peanuts, sardines and sausages

Science activity

Each can or packet of food has a label that tells you how much protein, carbohydrate, fat and vitamins there are in 100 grams of the food. Which food in your kitchen contains the most carbohydrate?

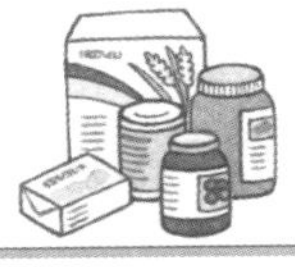

A balanced diet includes animal or plant protein, plenty of fresh fruit and vegetables, and energy coming mostly from carbohydrates rather than fats. Look at food labels with your child to find out the suggested daily intakes of vitamins and minerals.

13

What do animals eat?

Science facts
Many animals get the proteins, fats and carbohydrates they need by eating plants. These animals are called herbivores. Some animals catch and eat other animals. These meat eaters are called carnivores. Carnivores have special features to help them catch and kill other animals. These features may include sharp eyes that look to the front to help them see their prey.

Science quiz
The animals below are all carnivores. Draw a ring around the parts of each animal that help it catch and kill its prey.

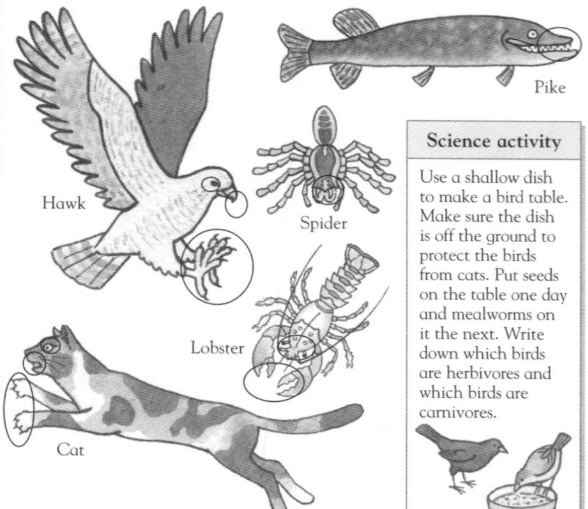

Science activity

Use a shallow dish to make a bird table. Make sure the dish is off the ground to protect the birds from cats. Put seeds on the table one day and mealworms on it the next. Write down which birds are herbivores and which birds are carnivores.

Most spiders have poor vision and rely on scents and vibrations to locate prey. Herbivores have features that give them protection against carnivores. Many have good eyesight and eyes on either side of the head to give them a wide field of vision.

14

What is a human skeleton?

Science facts
The human skeleton has about 206 bones. It supports and shapes the body and protects the soft internal organs.

Science quiz
Look at the picture and use the words in the box to complete the sentences.

Backbone	Elbow	Pelvis	Rib cage	Skull	Femur

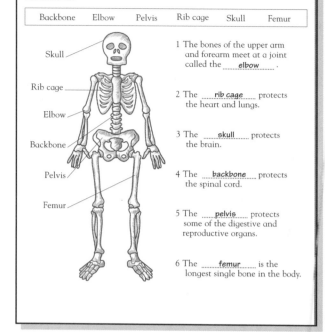

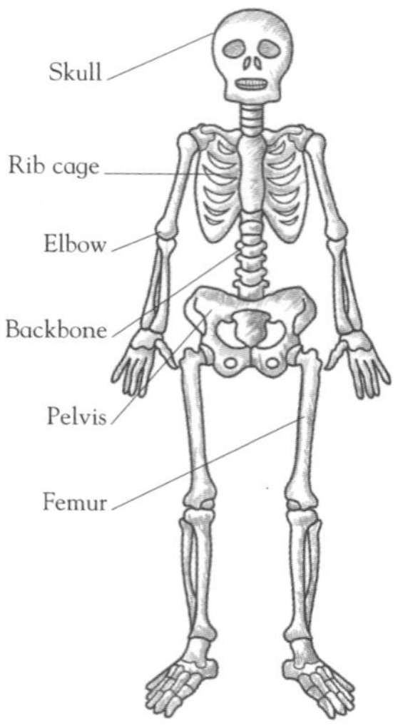

1 The bones of the upper arm and forearm meet at a joint called the ....elbow.... .

2 The ....rib cage.... protects the heart and lungs.

3 The ....skull.... protects the brain.

4 The ....backbone.... protects the spinal cord.

5 The ....pelvis.... protects some of the digestive and reproductive organs.

6 The ....femur.... is the longest single bone in the body.

Bones contain a spongy tissue called bone marrow. It produces red blood cells, white blood cells and platelets. Red blood cells transport oxygen, white blood cells fight infections and platelets help the blood clot whenever the body suffers a cut or bruise.

15

Do all animals have bones?

Science facts
Animals with bony skeletons inside them are called vertebrates. All vertebrates have a backbone. Vertebrates include humans, dogs, snakes, fish and birds. Skeletons give protection and support to the body and help it move. Animals, such as worms, insects, snails and jellyfish do not have bony skeletons; they are called invertebrates.

Science quiz
Here are the skeletons of a fish, a bird and a frog. On each of the drawings, colour in the part that protects the brain and colour in the backbone.

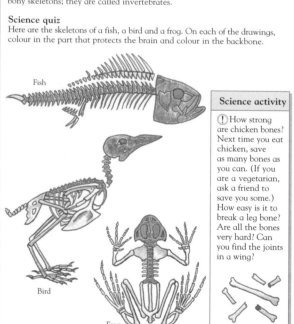

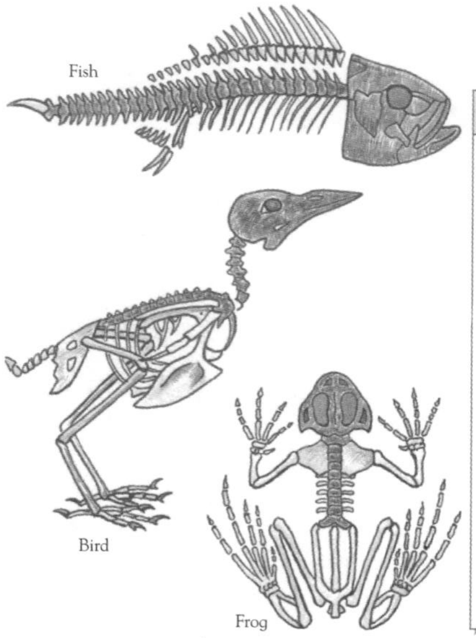

Science activity

(!) How strong are chicken bones? Next time you eat chicken, save as many bones as you can. (If you are a vegetarian, ask a friend to save you some.) How easy is it to break a leg bone? Are all the bones very hard? Can you find the joints in a wing?

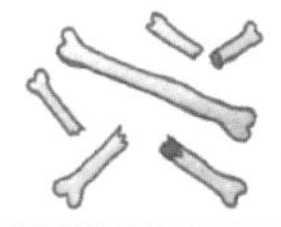

All animal skeletons protect the soft internal organs, provide anchor points for muscles and give rigidity and support to the body. As an extension to the *Science quiz*, ask your child to point out joints, where two or more bones meet in the body.

16

Where are your muscles?

Science facts
When muscles work, they get thicker and shorter. We say that the muscles contract. A contracting muscle pulls on a bone, making it move. There are muscles all over your body. Muscles need sugar and oxygen to work. They get both of these things from the blood. Most muscles rest after they have been used, but the heart muscle works non-stop throughout your life.

Science quiz
When you move your legs, feet, hands or arms, the muscles that move them get thicker and shorter.

On picture A, draw an arrow pointing to where you think the muscles moving the foot will get thicker.

On picture B, draw an arrow pointing to where you think the muscle raising the forearm will get thicker.

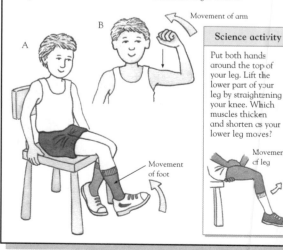

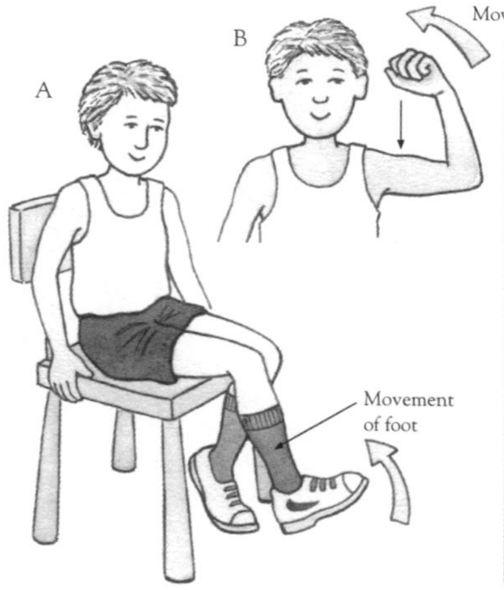

Science activity

Put both hands around the top of your leg. Lift the lower part of your leg by straightening your knee. Which muscles thicken and shorten as your lower leg moves?

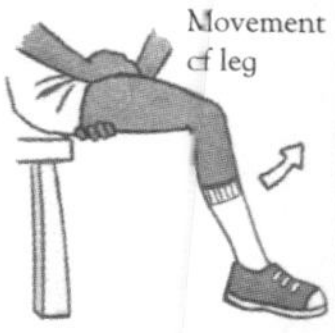

On this page, your child will learn that limbs move when muscles contract. By straightening the lower leg at the knee, your child will feel the thigh muscles contract and relax. Use a picture of a skeleton to show where these muscles attach to the body.

17

Is it a rock?

Science facts

Mountains, hills, cliffs, stones and pebbles are made of rock. Jewels are made of rock. Garden soil and sand are made up of many tiny bits of rock. There are many different types of rock. Some rocks are very hard; others are soft.

Science quiz

Colour all the different rocks you can see in this picture.

Science activity

Start a rock collection. But remember to ask an adult before you take any rocks from a beach or park. Are all your rocks the same colour?

Here, your child learns that there are different types of rock. You could visit a beach to find a variety of pebbles, and a jeweller's shop to see gemstones. Encourage your child to start a rock collection and to sort the rocks by colour.

18

What sort of rock is it?

Science facts

Rocks are very hard materials. Some rocks, called ores, contain metals. Others contain fossils of animals or plants that died millions of years ago. Many rocks contain crystals. A few rock crystals, such as diamond, are extremely valuable because they are very rare. These crystals are called gems. Some rocks, such as sandstone, are made when mud or grains of sand are slowly squashed together.

Science quiz

Use this Yes/No key to find the names of the rocks in the pictures.

Clue 1 Are there fossils in the rock? If yes, it is limestone. If there are no fossils to be seen, go to clue 2.

Clue 2 If there are crystals in the rock, go to clue 3. If there are no crystals in the rock, it is sandstone.

Clue 3 Are the crystals big? If yes, it is calcite. Are the crystals small? If yes, it is granite.

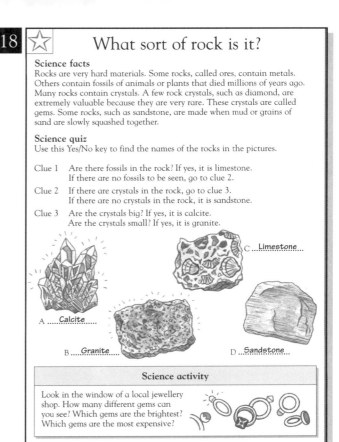

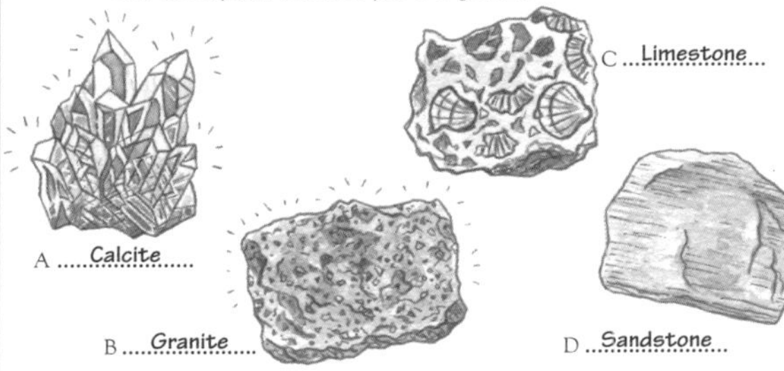
A ......Calcite......
B .....Granite.....
C ...Limestone...
D ..Sandstone..

Science activity

Look in the window of a local jewellery shop. How many different gems can you see? Which gems are the brightest? Which gems are the most expensive?

Your child will learn that rocks have different structures and textures. Some children find rocks a little dull, but they become excited by rocks that contain fossils. A fossil-hunting trip or a visit to a geological museum often inspires genuine interest.

19

Do rocks absorb water?

Science facts

Different types of rock are formed in different ways. Each type of rock has a different set of properties. One property of a rock is its porosity. This is the ability of the rock to absorb water. Water is held in rocks under the ground. The more porous the rock, the more water it can hold.

Science quiz

Some rocks were weighed. They were placed in water for an hour and then weighed again.

Rock	Weight before	Weight after
Granite	100 N	101 N
Chalk	50 N	100 N
Sandstone	100 N	150 N
Marble	75 N	76 N

Which rock absorbed the most water for its weight?

Chalk absorbed the most water for its weight. Its weight doubled.

What sorts of plant do you think will grow in areas where granite is the underlying rock? Use the chart above to help you answer this question.

Only plants that can survive in dry conditions grow in areas where granite is the underlying rock, as granite does not retain moisture.

Science activity

You can check the porosity of materials in a different way. Collect two different types of brick. Place each one in a bowl of shallow water and leave them for 30 minutes. Take them out and compare them by looking at how far the water has crept up each brick. Is one brick more porous than the other?

Most bricks absorb moisture. You could take this opportunity to discuss why we need to damp-proof brick buildings. If your home is made of brick, encourage your child to find out what material has been used to guard against dampness.

20

Which rock is this?

Science facts

There are many different types of rock. Some common rocks are granite, chalk, sandstone, limestone, flint and slate. They differ in the way they look and in their properties. Scientists often use keys to help identify rocks.

Science quiz

Use the Yes/No key below to identify these two rocks.

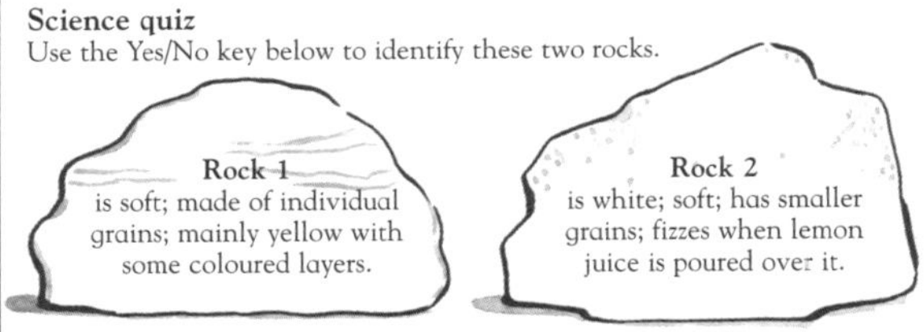
Rock 1
is soft; made of individual grains; mainly yellow with some coloured layers.
Rock 2
is white; soft; has smaller grains; fizzes when lemon juice is poured over it.

.........Sandstone......... ....Chalk.........

Key to some common rocks

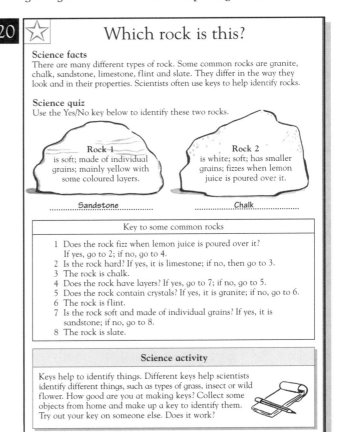

1 Does the rock fizz when lemon juice is poured over it? If yes, go to 2; if no, go to 4.
2 Is the rock hard? If yes, it is limestone; if no, then go to 3.
3 The rock is chalk.
4 Does the rock have layers? If yes, go to 7; if no, go to 5.
5 Does the rock contain crystals? If yes, it is granite; if no, go to 6.
6 The rock is flint.
7 Is the rock soft and made of individual grains? If yes, it is sandstone; if no, go to 8.
8 The rock is slate.

Science activity

Keys help to identify things. Different keys help scientists identify different things, such as types of grass, insect or wild flower. How good are you at making keys? Collect some objects from home and make up a key to identify them. Try out your key on someone else. Does it work?

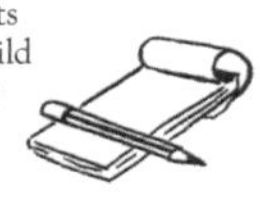

Help your child construct a key by asking questions that can divide things first into two sets, and then divide these sets into subsets, and so on. Encourage your child to try out his or her key and to see if others can make it work.

21 What is in the soil?

Science facts
Soil is made up mainly of small pieces, or particles, of rock. Tiny rock particles form mud when you add water to the soil. Soil can also contain slightly larger rock particles, such as sand grains. Heavier pieces of rock are called stones. Soil also contains humus (mainly rotted plant material).

Science quiz
Hannah dug some soil from her garden and put it into a plastic bottle with some water. She shook the bottle very hard until it was a muddy mixture, as shown in picture A. She left it for one hour and then came back to look at it again. Picture B shows what she saw.

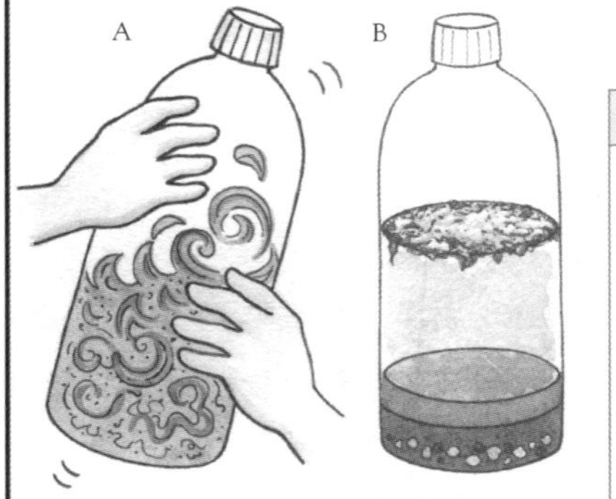

Bottle of shaken mud and water

Bottle after being left to stand for 1 hour

Can you explain what happened?
Larger, heavier particles settle on the bottom; smaller lighter particles settle on the top.

Science activity

(!) Look at soil with a magnifying glass. Can you see the different-sized particles? Is there any dead plant matter in the soil? Are there any tiny creatures in it? (Always wear gloves when handling soil.)

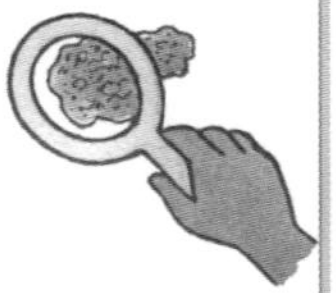

Tiny fragments are chipped off rocks when strong wind or fast-flowing water causes rocks to collide or when rocks split as they freeze or are heated up. These fragments gradually accumulate and mix with humus (dead plant material) to form soil.

22 Which soil holds water best?

Science facts
Different types of soil contain different sizes of rock particle. Soil with very fine particles is called silt or clay. Sandy soils contain slightly larger particles. Other soils contain lots of stones. Most soil is a mixture of all of these different-sized particles. The more sand and stones the soil contains, the easier it is for water to pass through the soil.

Science quiz
A class set up an experiment to find out which type of soil let the most water pass through it. One bottle held sandy soil, one held silt and clay, and one held a mixture of silt, clay and sand. The same amount of water was poured into each bottle. Holes in the bottom of each bottle let water passing through the soil drain into a beaker underneath. This is how they looked after 30 minutes.

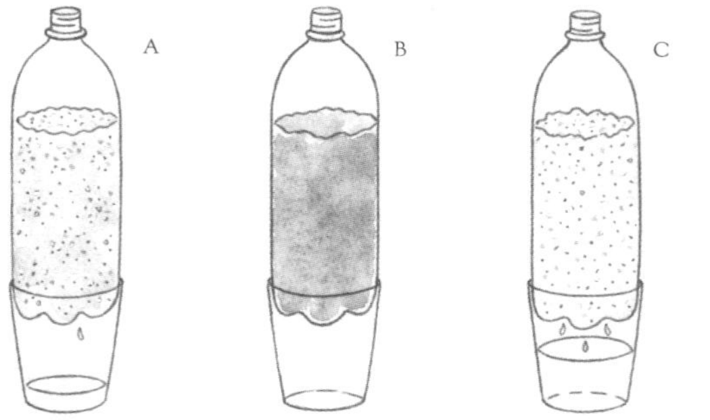

Which bottle contained the sandy soil? Bottle C

Science activity

(!) Try growing mung beans in a pot of garden soil. Do the same in pots of peat, compost and bulb fibre. In which material do the beans grow best? (Always wear gloves when handling garden soil.)

Water drains easily through the gaps between the sand particles. Fine silt and clay particles fit much closer together, trapping water in the tiny spaces between them. In the *Science activity*, let your child decide in advance what "grows best" will mean.

23 What kind of soil is this?

Science facts
Soil is made up of grains of broken rock and humus (mainly rotted plant material). A soil's type depends on the mix of humus and on the size of the grains of rock. The grains can be very small and smooth, such as in clay, or they can be larger, like grains of sand, pieces of gravel, or stones.

Science quiz
Use this key to identify the soil described below.

The soil is light in colour, gritty and drains well. The soil is sandy

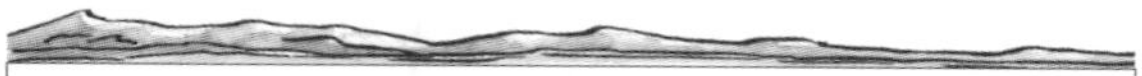

Does the soil feel gritty?
- Yes → Is the soil light in colour and does it drain very quickly?
  - Yes → Sandy
  - No → Loam
- No → Does the soil have very small grains and does it hold water?
  - Yes → Clay
  - No → Peat

Different plants prefer different types of soil. If a plant had roots that could rot very easily in water, which type of soil might help it grow well?
Sandy soil would drain water away from the roots and prevent them from rotting.

Science activity

(!) You can see the different parts that make up a soil by using water to separate them. Pour water into an empty jar until it is three-quarters full. Stir in three or four dessertspoons of soil and mix well. Allow time for the soil to settle so you can see the different parts. Try different soils. What do they look like?

After mixing water with soil, your child will see layers forming: the humus will float, the heavier grains will sink and the smaller clay particles will form an upper layer. The amount of each component will determine the type of soil.

24 Where does light come from?

Science facts
The light that we see with our eyes comes from objects called light sources. Light sources include the Sun, flames from candles and fires, and electric lamps. A few animals, such as fireflies, are light sources because they can make light inside their bodies. Light always travels in a straight line from a light source to our eyes. (Never look directly at the Sun, because its bright light can damage your eyes.)

Science quiz
The picture on the right shows how light from a fluorescent lamp reaches the eyes of the boy. Draw arrows to show how the light reaches the eyes of the children in the pictures below.

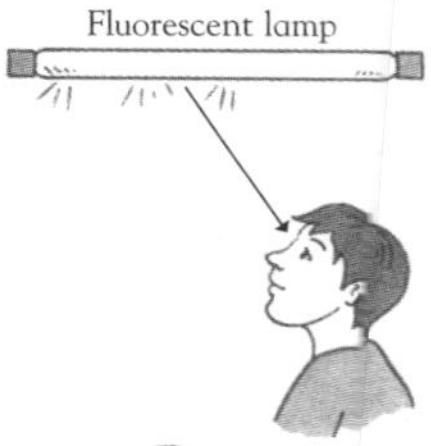

Science activity

(!) Try draping a duvet or some blankets over chairs and other furniture to make a very dark place where no light can get in. Take a torch into your dark place. This is your light source.

Light always travels in a straight line. We call the production of light by hot objects, such as the Sun, candles and light-bulb filaments, incandescence. Bioluminescence is the production of light by living things, such as fireflies, anglerfish and plankton.

25

Can you see through it?

Science facts
Materials that you can see clearly through, such as glass, are said to be transparent. Opaque materials, such as rock, are those that you cannot see through at all. You cannot see clearly through translucent materials, but if you hold a torch behind them you can see a bright patch of light.

Science quiz
Can you fill in the missing words in this table?

Material	Can you see through it?	Can you see torch light through it?	Scientific description
Aluminium kitchen foil	No	No.....	Opaque
Kitchen clingfilm	Yes	Yes	Transparent.
Greaseproof paper	No	Yes	Translucent.
Tissue paper	No.....	Yes...	Translucent
Cardboard	No	No	Opaque.........
Cotton handkerchief	No.....	Yes...	Translucent

Science activity

(!) Ask an adult to boil some water for you. Let the water cool and then use some of it to cover the bottom of a plastic container. In another plastic container, cover the bottom with tap water. Place both containers in a freezer and check them two or three hours later. Does the ice in the containers look different, and if so why?

Encourage your child to carry out the tests in the *Science quiz* to find out the correct answers. In the *Science activity*, freezing boiled water produces more transparent ice because tiny air bubbles, which cause clouding, have been boiled out of the water.

26

Where is the shadow?

Science facts
You cannot see through objects that are opaque because light will not pass through them. When you put an opaque object between a light source and a wall, a dark area called a shadow forms on the wall. The shadow forms because the object stops light from reaching the wall. Remember that light always travels in straight lines.

Science quiz
Mina taped a cardboard circle to a drinking straw. Then she held the circle in front of a shining torch, so that a shadow formed on the wall. Can you draw the shadow that formed on the wall?

Science activity

Use a torch to form a shadow of an object on a wall. What happens to the shadow when you move the torch nearer to the object? What happens to the shadow when you move the object closer to the wall?

Your child will learn that shadows are formed by the absence of light. In the *Science activity*, the shadow is enlarged by moving the torch nearer to the object. Moving the object nearer to the screen makes the shadow smaller.

27

What makes things shiny?

Science facts
Shiny objects have very smooth surfaces, which reflect light especially well. These objects reflect a lot of light into our eyes, making them appear shiny.

Science quiz
The picture on the right shows how light reflects off a shiny ring and into the girl's eyes. Use a ruler to draw arrows that show how the light reflects off these shiny things into the eyes of the children.

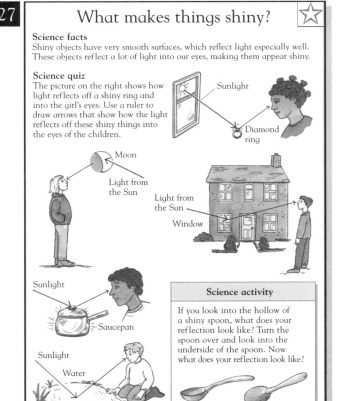

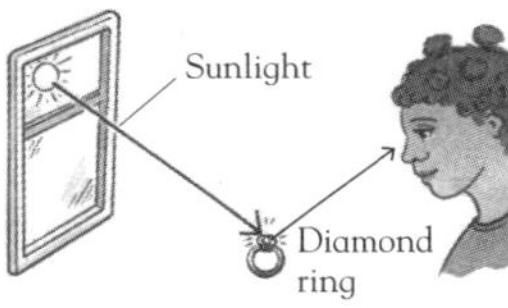
Sunlight
Diamond ring

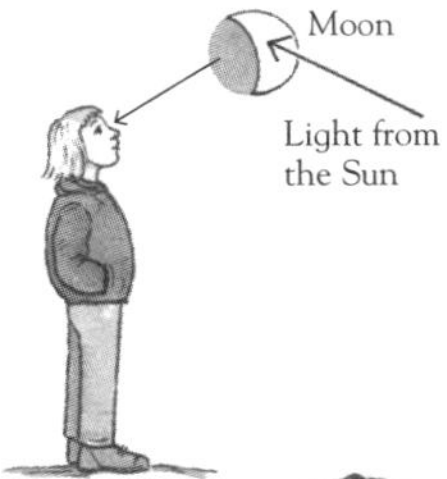
Moon
Light from the Sun

Light from the Sun
Window

Sunlight
Saucepan

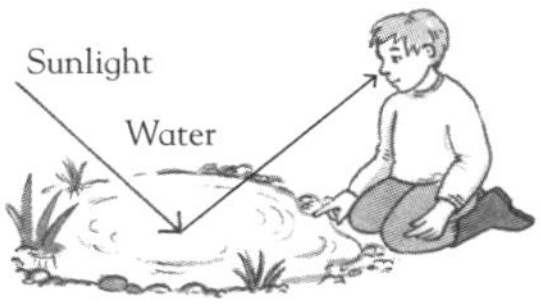
Sunlight
Water

Science activity

If you look into the hollow of a shiny spoon, what does your reflection look like? Turn the spoon over and look into the underside of the spoon. Now what does your reflection look like?

When we see ordinary objects, only some of the light that reflects off them enters our eyes; the rest is scattered in other directions. Some objects and surfaces direct much more of the reflected light into our eyes, making them appear shiny.

28

Is it a push or a pull?

Science facts
Forces can make things move. Pushes and pulls are examples of forces that make things move. Magnets push and pull each other because they have a force called magnetism. The Earth pulls things downwards with a force called gravity. Squashes are pushes that make objects change shape.

Science quiz
The pictures show a number of forces in action. Decide whether each force is a push, a pull or a squash. Write your answer beside each picture.

This force is a .....push.....
This force is a ...squash...
This force is a ..squash....
This force is a ......pull......
This force is a .....push.....
This force is a ......pull......

Science activity

Try pushing against bathroom scales. The scales will show you how hard you are pushing. Can you push harder with your hand or your finger? Does a leg push harder than an arm? Who is the best pusher in your family?

It is relatively easy for children to understand that pushes and pulls are forces. It's harder to grasp that stretching, bending, turning and squashing are also examples of forces in action, usually produced by the combined effects of two or more forces.

29 Is the surface rough or smooth?

Science facts
When you kick a ball, it starts moving then gradually slows down until it stops. The force that makes the ball slow down is called friction. Friction is a force between two surfaces that are touching, such as the surface of a ball and the ground. Rough surfaces produce more friction than smooth ones.

Science quiz
Mary and Sean rolled marbles down a tube and measured how far each marble rolled. They tried rolling the marbles over different surfaces. They kept the angle of the tube the same each time. Here are their results.

Surface	Distance marble rolls
Gravel path	21 cm
Grass	3 cm
Kitchen floor	163 cm
Carpet	32 cm
Pavement	85 cm

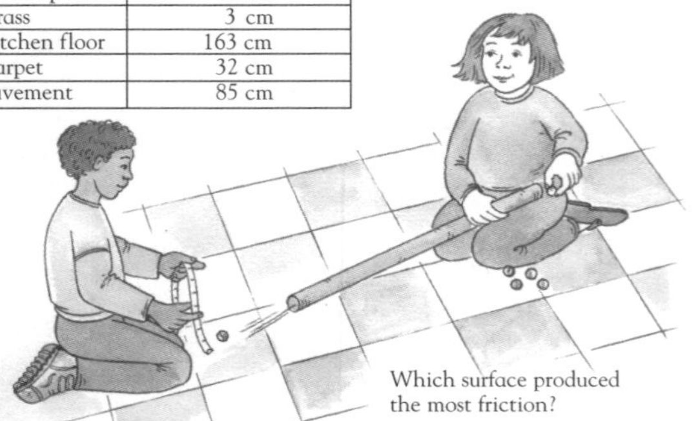

Which surface produced the most friction?
......Grass......

Science activity

Slide coins down a slightly tilted table top or wooden board. Wet the surface a little and try sliding the coins down it again. Is a dry or wet surface best for sliding? Which surface produces the most friction?

When two surfaces are in contact, friction acts to prevent one surface from moving over the other, no matter how smooth they are. In the *Science activity*, the surface should be tilted at the same angle each time. The wet surface produces the least friction.

30 Is it attracted to a magnet?

Science facts
A magnet will try to pull some metal objects towards itself. We say that the magnet attracts these objects. Magnets will attract only objects containing the metals iron, steel, cobalt or nickel. They will not attract other metals.

Science quiz
Draw a line from the magnet to each of the metal objects it will attract.

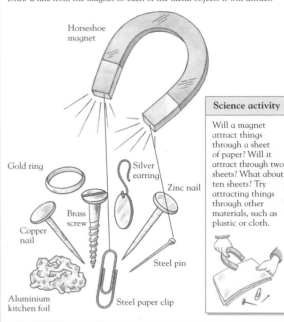

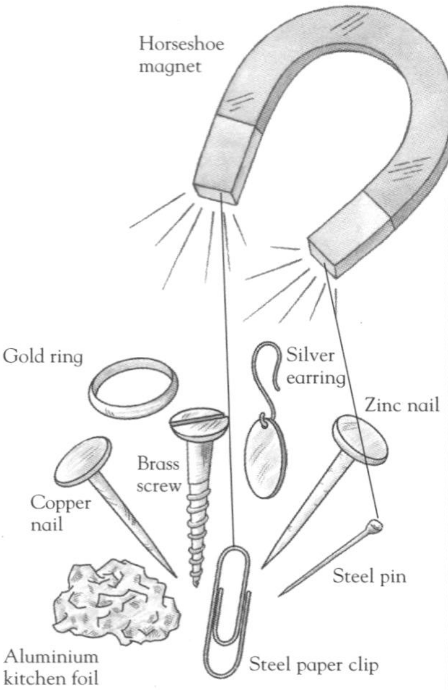

Science activity

Will a magnet attract things through a sheet of paper? Will it attract through two sheets? What about ten sheets? Try attracting things through other materials, such as plastic or cloth.

Magnets exert an invisible force called magnetism. The area in which a magnet exerts this force is its magnetic field. Metals that are attracted to magnets or that can be made into magnets, such as iron, steel or cobalt, are said to be magnetic.

31 Which is the best magnet?

Science facts
The most common magnets we see are those that stick to refrigerator doors. Magnets can be many different shapes and sizes. Some are horseshoe shaped. Others are shaped like rings, bars, discs and rods. Some magnets are very strong and attract things from a long way away.

Science quiz
Each of these magnets was dipped into a box of steel paper clips. Put a tick (✔) below the strongest magnet.

Science activity

Stroke a metal coat hanger repeatedly with the end of a bar magnet. Always stroke in the same direction and lift the magnet away from the coat hanger between strokes. You will find that the coat hanger becomes a magnet, too. Will the coat hanger pick up as many steel paper clips as the bar magnet?

Your child will learn that some magnets are stronger than others. When a magnet comes into contact with a paper clip, the clip also turns into a magnet. This is called induced magnetism and it is what happens to the coat hanger in the *Science activity*.

32 Do they attract or repel?

Science facts
On every magnet, there are two areas where the magnetism is strongest. These areas are called the magnet's north and south poles. A north pole of one magnet will always attract the south pole of another magnet. However, if two north poles or two south poles are placed together, they will push each other apart. These magnets repel each other.

Science quiz
Look at the pairs of magnets shown in the pictures. Which pairs will attract each other? Which pairs will repel each other? Circle the right answers.

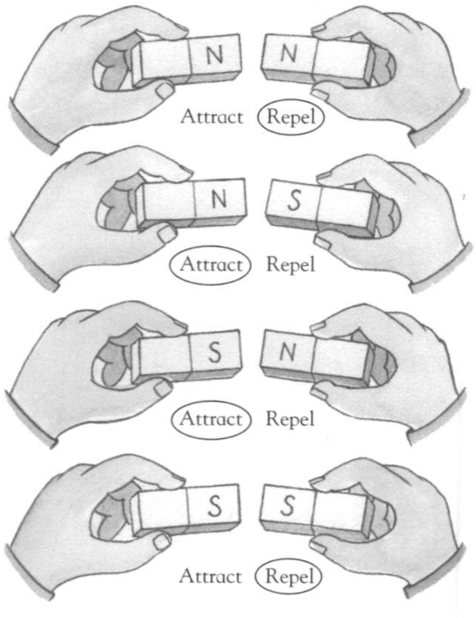

Science activity

How could you stack a pile of bar magnets? Make a drawing of the pile, marking the north poles with the letter **N** and the south poles with the letter **S**.

The principle is that like poles repel, while unlike poles attract. When you cut a magnet in half, each half becomes a magnet with its own north and south poles. Bar magnets have to be stacked with north poles above south, and south above north.